# UNITED NATIONS

## FOR BEGINNERS

# BY IAN WILLIAMS

# WRITERS AND READERS PUBLISHING, INC.

P.O. BOX 461, VILLAGE STATION
NEW YORK, NY 10014

WRITERS AND READERS LIMITED
9 CYNTHIA STREET
LONDON N1 9JF
ENGLAND

Copyright © 1995 Ian Williams
Cover Design © 1995 Terrie Dunkelberger
Book Design by Paul Gordon

A Writers and Readers Documentary Comic Book Copyright © 1995

ISBN # 0-86316-185-5

0 1 2 3 4 5 6 7 8 9

Manufactured in the United States of America

Beginners Documentary Comic Books are published by Writers and Readers
Publishing, Inc. Its trademark, consisting of the words "For Beginners, Writers and
Readers Documentary Comic Books" and the Writers and Readers logo, is regis-
tered in the U.S. Patent and Trademark
Office and in other countries.

# UNITED NATIONS

## FOR BEGINNERS

# CONTENTS

# CONTENTS

## Introduction -

# A GOOD IDEA FALLEN AMONG THIEVES

The UN has the media relations of a 1950s state bureaucracy. It doesn't like reporters looking into its inner workings, and it threatens dire penalties to staff found leaking information to the media.

Time and time again, when journalists have exposed scandals in the UN, senior officials have set up an enquiry - into who leaked!

What UN bureaucrats prefer, and what they often get, is "groupie" reporting, on how wonderful the UN is. And I thought so too...at first.

**My main objection to it was that it was so boring. Then I discovered that beyond the event horizon in that gray hole on the East River, all sorts of interesting things were happening.**

By now, the greatest hope for the UN's survival as a worthwhile organization rests with some of its huge staff, at all levels, who could be dismissed under staff rules. These people care enough about the organization to leak to journalists.

UN CHARTER

*Press leak as seen by some UN officials...*

They realize that their superiors won't reform the organization, nor promote justice, unless prodded from outside. They think the organization stands for more than a big salary and guaranteed promotion and pension.

With this book I want to UNravel the UN I want to explain how it *should* work and how it *does* work. I *like* the notion of a world organization but have serious reasons to question the idea that national governments - even the one in Washington - know best.

So that's why I also dedicate this book to "the peoples of the world," whose United Nations it should really be.

# THE UN FOR ABSOLUTE BEGINNERS

**THE UNITED NATIONS IS VERY SIMPLE -**
*AND VERY COMPLICATED*
**AT THE SAME TIME.**

# THE SIMPLE QUESTIONS AND ANSWERS ARE:

| | |
|---|---|
| **WHEN?** | 1945. |
| **WHAT?** | Six organs and dozens of agencies and programmes. |
| **WHERE?** | New York... and Vienna and Geneva and Nairobi and Paris and so on. |
| **WHO?** | 185 governments. |
| **WHY?** | To stop war. |
| **HOW?** | With persuasion, sanctions, and collective military action. |

But while simple questions and answers are nice, the real world is neither nice nor simple. So we'll just have to expand.

# WHEN?

On 26 June 1945, representatives of 51 countries meeting in San Francisco signed the Charter of the United Nations.

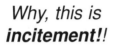

*Why, this is* **incitement!!**

The document was considered so precious that when it was flown to Washington, it was attached to a parachute. The bearer, Alger Hiss, had to take his own chances.

It began:

## "WE THE PEOPLES OF THE WORLD, DETERMINED

to save succeeding generations from the scourge of war, which twice in our life time has brought untold sorrow to mankind, and

to reaffirm faith in fundamental human rights, in the dignity and worth of the human person, in the equal rights of men and women and of nations large and small and

to establish conditions under which peace and justice and respect for the obligations arising from treaties and other sources of international law can be maintained, and to promote social progress and better standards of life in larger freedom,

continued...

**AND FOR THESE ENDS**
to practice tolerance, and live together in peace with one another as good neighbours, and

to unite our strength to maintain international peace and security, and

to ensure, by the acceptance of principles and the institution of methods, that armed force shall not be used, save in the common interest, and to employ international machinery for the promotion of the economic and social advancement of all peoples,

**HAVE RESOLVED TO COMBINE OUR EFFORTS TO ACCOMPLISH THESE AIMS.**

Accordingly, our respective Governments, through representatives assembled in the city of San Francisco, who have exhibited their full powers found to be in good and due form, have agreed to the present Charter of the United Nations, and do hereby establish an international organization to be known as the United Nations."

What about the rights of the military juntas?!?

Stirring stuff - but during the drafting conference, the US's first African-American diplomat, Ralph Bunche confided to his diary: "There is practically no inspiration out here - every nation is dead set on looking out for its own national self-interest." Things haven't changed much!

Even so, it's a stirring document, on a par with the United States Declaration of Independence and the British Magna Carta as a symbol of human aspirations. The lofty sentiments are not always honoured, but the fact that over 185 governments have signed it, gives support to all those who struggle for a better life - often against those very governments.

"The Charter of the United Nations is the first, most daring code of behaviour addressed to the most powerful of all institutions of the planet— armed nations."

-- U Thant, from Burma, first Third World Secretary General, 1961--1971

# WHY?

*1945 AND ALL THAT*

*Originally, the winning side in World War II used the name "The United Nations" to distinguish themselves from the "Axis" powers: Germany, Italy, and Japan.*

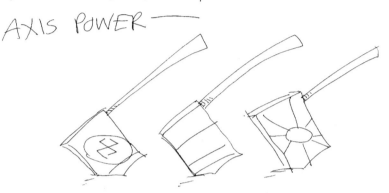

AXIS POWER —

Many of those who suffered in the war were veterans of the First World War, which had ended with the resounding cry "Never Again!" By 1945, they were adding, "And this time we mean it!"

They wanted an organization that would make sure that there would be no more wars. The leaders of the Allies did a lot of declaring in the process, but it was resounding stuff.

"In the future days, which we seek to make secure, we look forward to a world founded upon four essential freedoms.
The first is freedom of speech and expression - everywhere in the world.
The second is freedom of every person to worship God in his own way - everywhere in the world.
The third is freedom from want ...
The fourth is freedom from fear."

-- President Franklin D. Roosevelt,
6 January 1941

*(Of course, we are all still looking forward to this!)*

In London in June 1941, before Japan attacked the US at Pearl Harbour, the countries fighting against Germany and Italy signed the "London Declaration" that their purpose was to establish a "world in which, relieved of the menace of aggression, all may enjoy economic and social security."

One of the early shapers of the UN was Alger Hiss. He later fell foul of the House un-American Activities Committee as a suspected Communist. (Like in the old witch trials, suspicion was enough evidence in most cases.)

As almost a proto-General Secretary, his team from the OSS -the forerunner of the CIA - designed the UN flag and insignia. The original model was a logo based on the OSS's design for delegate passes in San Francisco - a white globe on blue back-

ground, seen from the North. The final version, adopted in January 1946, used the Greenwich meridian through Britain as the centre axis.

Behind the high-falutin' rhetoric there was some serious old- fashioned horse-trading. At the Yalta Conference in 1944, British Prime Minister Winston Churchill, U.S. President Franklin D. Roosevelt and Soviet leader Joseph Stalin sat down and drew the shape of the modern world, without going out of their way to ask what the locals thought about it all.

They drew lines on maps that were soon marked on the ground by barbed wire and minefields.

Despite the plots of their leaders, the war-weary peoples of the world wanted an organization that would guarantee speedy and effective action against any new Hitlers or Mussolinis.

*"Actually, no, I don't think I really want to play war today."*

"There has never been a war which, if the facts had been put calmly before the ordinary folk, could not have been prevented. The common man is the greatest protection against war."

-- Ernest Bevin, who began his working life as a docker and became Britain's Labour Foreign Minister in 1945.

The main purpose of the organization is, in the Charter's words, "to save succeeding generations from the scourge of war." So it is a World Government? If aliens landed and said, "take me to your leader," would you direct them to New York?

No way! As **Secretary General Boutros Boutros - Ghali** said despairingly,

"I am not a country of 50 million people. I have no army. I have no land, no police. The importance of the United Nations comes from its moral value, its credibility."

Mostly, the UN does what its 185 member governments tell it to do. Some of those governments are democratic, some are not; some are humanitarian, some viciously inhumane. Most of them resent the idea of "peoples" bypassing them to speak to the rest of the world. It can't even enforce its decisions against a member unless enough countries are prepared to take action.

"There is nothing wrong with the United Nations - except its governments."

-- **Lord Caradon**, Britain's Delegate to the UN, 1964-70

Historians argue whether it was Churchill or Roosevelt who thought up the name "the United Nations." Others say it was neither-- probably the poet, Lord Byron.

But the author of the words, "We the peoples," was almost certainly Field Marshal Jan Smuts, who had also helped found the League of Nations. He was trying to say the same thing as Ralph Bunche, who declared, "There are no warlike peoples - just warlike leaders."

However, Smuts was also Prime Minister of South Africa, where at the time, most Africans had no vote. So just who were these "peoples"? By 1945, Smuts had begun to question the racism of the white South Africans he represented back home, just as they began to adopt Apartheid as the official system. Smuts couldn't turn the tide back home, but the UN did almost 50 years later!

# WHAT?

The UN has six main organs. But it is a very strange animal, since it has no arms. At different times, different organs have been more important than others - and at least one of them is now totally obsolete:

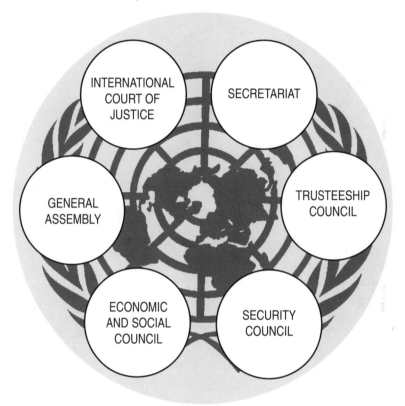

And attached to them are a whole
alphabet soup of agencies dealing
with different fields of work
(or not, as the case sometimes is).

# THE GENERAL ASSEMBLY

The core of the United Nations is the General Assembly, where all 185 member countries have one vote each. **The Pacific Island state of Palau with 15,000 people has the same voting strength as China or India with their billions.**

It can meet and vote on any subject, unless the Security Council is dealing with it (or at least pretending to). However its decisions only carry moral force - unlike the Council's, they're not binding in international law. But the Assembly votes are an important opinion poll on how and what the majority of the world thinks about issues.

That was shown in 1992 and 1993 when the Assembly voted that the Arms Embargo on the Bosnian government should be lifted. The Security Council, armed with the vetoes of the British, French, and Russians, ignored it.

"Important questions" need a two -- thirds vote of the Assembly to pass. The question of what is an important question *isn't* important. It's decided by the delegates themselves - by a simple majority.

The General Assembly controls the purse strings of the organization. Officially, at least. It decides the budget and staffing levels of the organization and the various peacekeeping missions that the Security Council sets up. (Sometimes the U.S. Congress forgets that, and thinks that it should decide for the rest of the world!)

"I settle more problems and do more business in one week at the UN General Assembly than in three months of travel round the world."

-- Henry Kissinger, former US Secretary of State during the Viet Nam war.

## The Case of the Delegate Who Didn't Talk!

In 1989, the Bhutanese delegate set an example which, alas, has never been followed. Towards the end of the "general debate" of the General Assembly, when everyone was generally bored, he was the last-scheduled speaker at the end of a very long, hot and humid day. He cast his eyes around the audience and told them that since they had written copies of his speech, it would be silly to make them listen to him read it! Some delegates claimed that if he'd run for President of the Assembly, he'd have won in perpetuity!

In fact, even though there are now three times as many delegates as in 1945, and the world is a much more complicated place, the General Assembly meets for the same period of time as it did in the 40s, when its termination was fixed by the time of the last steamships to get to Europe before Christmas!

The Assembly also votes on the Security Council's recommendation for Secretary General - but it can't make its own nominations. It also elects 10 of the 15 members of the Security Council for two- year terms.

The delegates get together in regional groupings to vote for positions. In addition to these regional groups, there is a Group of 77 -- with 134 members! -- representing the developing nations (the UN has different mathematics, as well as different language from the rest of us).

The Non-Aligned Movement, with 111 members, continues to meet even now that, with the end of the Cold War, **no one is sure exactly who it is that they're not aligned with.**

In the basement, the **Francophone Group** meets regularly to plot the downfall of English -- *en Francais, naturellement.*

The President of the General Assembly is elected by the members on annual basis. With the passion for rotation (otherwise known as going round in circles) in the UN, each regional group takes it in turn, and the tradition has developed that each country can only take the Presidency once until all have had their turn.

**The General Assembly** (GA) deputes its work to six committees which, with all the imagination we have come to associate with UN diplomats, are called the First, Second, Third, Fourth, Fifth, and Sixth Committees.

The **First** deals with **Disarmament**;
the **Second** with **Economic** and **Financial** matters;
the **Third** with **Social Humanitarian** and **Cultural** matters;
the **Fourth** with **Decolonization**;
the **Fifth** with **Administrative** and **Budgetary** affairs;
and the **Sixth** with **Legal Matters**.

And of course there are others, with increasingly punishing names that make the reader long for the simplicity of numbers. Try the Advisory Committee on Administrative and Budgetary Questions (ACABQ) for size.

Some critics complain that the GA has too many "outdated resolutions." You know right away that that country wishes the resolution would go away for reasons other than their age.

OUTDATED RESOLUTION

For example, the U.S. said this often about resolutions on Palestinian refugees - but they are still refugees after 48 years. The longest lasting resolutions were those condemning Apartheid in South Africa - which of course was only *really* outdated in 1994 when Nelson Mandela became President in Pretoria.

Fidel Castro

In fact, most of the world often disagrees with what passes for political certainty in Washington! For example, the resolutions criticizing the US Embargo on Cuba are regularly overlooked in the American press.

With its efforts towards international treaties and agreements on human rights, the environment, and similar issues, the Assembly actually does a lot of unspectacular but useful work.

On the other hand, many UN members feel that the Security Council does the opposite: a lot of spectacular but useless work, since the great powers can and do stop anything that threatens their interests.

The UN *does do* some useful work that doesn't hit the headlines. For example, under the Charter, all international treaties have to be deposited with the United Nations, which keeps a record of signatures, of ratifications, and of countries which withdraw their signatures.

So what? Well, secret treaties played a big part in the lead up to both World War I and II. Of course countries still make secret agreements - but we have the small consolation that they're not legally binding.

# THE SECURITY COUNCIL

Ignoring the Assembly, the media and politicians now focus almost entirely on the Security Council, where sexy issues like war and peace are decided. To deter all would-be aggressors, the Security Council—under Chapter VII of the Charter—has the right to call upon all UN members, first to impose sanctions, and then "such action by air, sea or land forces as may be necessary."

Perhaps under the influence of H.G. Wells, whose *Shape of Things to Come* had anticipated world peace being kept by an air police force, Article 45 of the Charter says,

> **"Members shall hold immediately available national air-force contingents for combined international enforcement action."** However, it was a concept which never took off.

## The Famous Five

As we saw, ten members are picked from the Assembly for two-year terms, according to Article 23, "due regard being specially paid" to their contribution to maintaining the peace as well as "equitable geographical distribution."

That has been a total dead letter because of the **"Buggin's turn"** principle. In 1992 the crumbling kleptocracy of Zaire was a member, along with Morocco, which was still occupying the Western Sahara in contravention of Security Council resolutions. In 1994, Rwanda was represented by the government which was busily massacring hundreds of thousands back home.
So was tiny Djibouti.

That gives even more advantage to the other five "Permanent Members" - the great powers (as of 1945 at least), Britain, China, France, Russia, and the USA. Even though the balance of power has shifted a little in fifty years, **a "no" vote by any one of them can stop any resolution, even if the other 14 are in favour.**

They made one small concession many years ago when they graciously decided that an abstention wouldn't count as a veto, although the Charter itself says an *affirmative vote of*

the five is necessary. To pass, a resolution needs nine "yes" votes of the Council.

Although the world has changed a lot since the vetoes were Chartered, the only way to change is by amending the Charter, which needs a two-thirds vote of the Assembly. But even there the Famous Five can veto any amendment.

CURB YOUR HOSTILITIES

UN SECURITY COUNCIL ENTRANCE

Most of the substantial business is now dealt with in private consultations, closed to the media, and some diplomats claim that most questions are now decided by the P3, (Britain, France, and the US), who then take it to the P4 (P3 plus Russia), and then to the P5, which includes China.

**(P3+1) +1 = P5 = Piss Off!**

In fact, there's still some horse trading, particularly with the Non-Aligned bloc members. Some of them can be counted upon to bow to Western pressure, and all are aware of the veto, so the type of compromise that emerges is pretty much what you'd expect if a group of 5 heavily armed people negotiated with ten unarmed civilians.

On the Security Council the Presidency rotates monthly in (English) alphabetic order of country names. Each month as the Presidency changes, every delegate who speaks at the full meeting, heaps fulsome and usually insincere praise on the previous President, and equally unctuously welcomes the incoming President. This is, of course, done in public - all the important business is done in private.

After the Gulf War, no one wanted to provoke or humiliate the world's last superpower. So the device that was adopted to show displeasure without risking a veto was Presidential Statements. These are utterly meaningless in international law and have no authority on anyone. But they do show the folks back home that "something" was being done.

# Veto Power

THANK YOU FOR NOT USING YOUR POWER OF THE VETO

SECURITY COUNCIL

*"No" Score TableSco*

**USSR - 116.** including two for Russia in 1993 and in 1994 (both on obscure issues), so everyone assumed they were just flexing their muscles to show their irritation at being taken for granted.

**USA - 70.** The USA used to pride itself on not using the veto even though it was their invention, since they did not like the idea of US troops under foreign (i.e., UN) command. The first American veto was cast under Richard Nixon's administration, and the second was cast by future President George Bush, who was then US envoy to the UN They soon made up for lost time.

**Britain - 30.** This includes the memorable occasion in 1956 when they vetoed an American resolution on Suez.

**France - 18.** Like London, Paris is increasingly reluctant to say "non" in case anyone asks questions about the great power status of the two imperial has beens.

**China - 3.** Until 1974, the Chinese were represented by the Nationalist government in Taiwan, and they prefer to abstain on most issues on which they disagree. The old Taiwanese vetoed the admission of Mongolia in 1955, since, although they didn't control mainland China, if they did, they would claim Mongolia was part of it. The People's Republic later added two nays, leaving the Chinese both absolutely per capita the most undervetoed permanent member.

Nikita Khrushchev

Although the veto is resented by everyone who doesn't have it, there is a pragmatic justification for it. In the years after World War II, the veto stopped the organization from urinating into a gale, trying to thwart the Great Powers over whom it could exercise little or no influence.

Later, by an unhappy coincidence, the Permanent Five just happened to be the states with a declared weapon even greater than the veto - they all had nuclear bombs.

> **"No country without an atom bomb could properly consider itself independent."**
>
> -- Charles De Gaulle - the French President who could say "non" - and often did.

*"Enough small talk, gentlemen... Let's get down to some war mongering."*

Perhaps that even justifies the fact that most of the American vetoes have been exercised, not on behalf of America itself, but of Israel -- a state that everyone else presumes has a substantial nuclear arsenal -- even though it denies it.

In 1945, everyone assumed that the Permanent Five would stick together and beat up on anyone who rocked the boat. Instead, they got the Cold War. Then, the Charter assumed that the Five would use conventional methods to do so.

Instead, within months Hiroshima and Nagasaki disintegrated into radioactive mushroom clouds. This would prove that the "scourge of war " invoked in the Charter was even worse than everyone had first thought, and that it took more than signatures on a piece of paper to banish it.

"The UN Charter is thus a pre-atomic age document. In this sense it was obsolete before it actually came into force."

-- John Foster Dulles 1953, US Secretary of State, 1953

As the Cold War froze on, the UN settled into one of its most useful roles - the official scapegoat of the world. The countries that cause the problems can always blame the world body for its failure to deal with them!

We'll see later why that happened.

# SECRETARIES GENERAL

*--"If I ruled the world!"*

**The Secretary General (SG) is an organ of the UN! He (or she, sometime?) is elected every five years.**

For those five years, he runs the UN as an autocrat. Officially the Security Council nominates him to the General Assembly - which *could* vote it down. In the Council, each of the five permanent members can veto any nomination. So even if 14 other Council members and 185 General Assembly members wanted someone, it just takes one of the Five to block him or, we should be so lucky, her.

After a lot of horse trading, the famous Five have usually agreed on the lowest common denominator, someone who is the least offensive to all of them, not a citizen of any of their countries, and guaranteed to be pliant and sycophantic while running a 50,000 strong organization.

## What We Wanted!

During W.W.II, former League of Nations officials drew up a paper outlining the requirements for the SG of the future UN.

They said he should be "young. Political or diplomatic experience, but not necessarily great fame or eminence. Above all, ability for administration in the broadest sense is important, implying a knowledge of when to force an issue and be dynamic; when at the other extreme, to be content as a purely administrative official; and when on a middle course to be a moderator...."

In addition, they said he should at all times have "common sense, courage, integrity, and tact."

# What We Got!

Ever since, the Security Council has taken this as a negative example, so they usually nominate people who are closer to their second childhood than to youth, and who make the Lion in the Wizard of Oz seem positively reckless.

Dag Hammarskjöld was the closest to the specifications - but as we'll see later, **he was a mistake.**

"*Your card says:* BE SECRETARY GENERAL FOR A DAY -- *You must keep the peace, try to end hunger and balance the UN budget without upsetting any of the member states or staff...*"

Article 98 allows the Assembly, Security Council, and other organs to entrust the Secretary General with "other functions," and more importantly Article 99 allows him to take matters which he considers threaten "international peace and security" to the Security Council.

That means that an effective Secretary General has to be able to grandstand when necessary, to force governments to take notice of the principles he represents. But he must also be the perfect diplomat, an almost invisible intermediary, and at the same time an administrator.

## Protocol

Secretary-General
Boutros Boutros-Ghali

To an outsider, it may seem that the UN Secretary General is a sort of shadow President of the World. But in protocol terms for most Western countries he is merely a super envoy, and only has the privileges of a Foreign Minister.

According to the UN he is equivalent to a Prime Minister. But if you have a Secretary General visiting your home, the way to his heart, is to give him a 21 gun salute as if he were a head of state, which is what most Third World countries do.

It is hardly surprising that Hammarskjöld once said that the job was like a Secular Pope - without the Church. And it might be said, unlike the Pope, he has no state to represent him.

But for his church, the Secretary General has the Secretariat, the staff. To make sure that the UN has a truly international-ist staff, not serving the interests of their home countries, the Charter includes two articles, 100 and 101, which have the rare distinction of being the two most frequently flouted articles in a much flouted document.

Article 100 says that staff "shall not seek or receive instruction from any government or from any other authority exter-nal to the Organization," and pledges all members to "respect the exclusively international character of the responsibilities of the Secretary General and the staff and not to seek to influence them in the dis-charge of their responsi-bilities."

Article 101 says, opti-mistically, "The paramount consideration in the employment of the staff ... shall be the necessity of securing the highest stan-dards of efficiency, compe-tence, and integrity. Due regard shall be paid to the importance of recruiting the staff on as wide a geo-graphical basis as possi-ble."

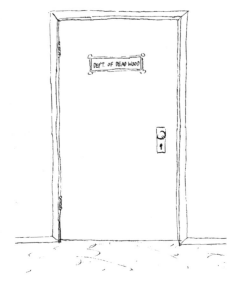

In fact, right from the beginning, the top jobs have been "gifts" to various governments, and even lesser appointments are the subject of incessant lobbying by governments that don't always consider quality to be important. In a way, the surprise is that so many people remained dedicated to the ideals of the UN under such pressures.

# The Staff

*—Professional pen-pushers and peacemakers and generally serviceable types*

Staff are divided into two groups: Professionals, who are supposed to be available for worldwide service anywhere; and General Service, who do the clerical and manual work. In all, there are supposed to be 51,484 Professionals and General Service staff.

(There are many more if you don't forget the 18,000 local employees of United Nations Relief and Work Agency [UNRWA], which has for fifty years been the biggest employer of Palestinians in the world. But they usually are forgotten, especially when one of the Middle Eastern governments arrests or harasses them.)

If you include their families, the UN "Nation" is more populous than many of its members. Many people think that there are too many staff in the UN, that it's a bloated bureaucracy. To put it in perspective, in 1994, New York State had almost twice as many lawyers (95,764) as the UN has staff.

Their pay and promotion scales are decided by the International Civil Service Commission, which bases their rates on the highest paid civil servants in the world - which used to be the US Federal Government, but no longer. American staff at the UN pay income tax - the rest pay a "staff assessment," which is set against their governments' contributions.

## A common joke in the UN

Q: "How many people work here?"
A: Oh, about half!"

# THE ECONOMIC AND SOCIAL COUNCIL

### World Social Security? Call ECOSOC!
EcoSoc isn't some ecologically sound footwear.

It's the Economic and Social Council- and it's the Cinderella of the organization. Instead of dealing with sexy items like wars and massacres, EcoSoc's 54 members are supposed to look after the mundane business of development, feeding, and culture. Which is why no one outside ever hears from it.

The UN founders knew that the Crash and Depression had played big parts in the rise of Nazism and in the rush to war. They wanted to avert such problems at their earliest stages.

But the International Monetary Fund and the World Bank picked up and ran away with many of the most important functions of EcoSoc. They were under the control of industrialized countries, so while EcoSoc's membership expanded to 54, its real power shrank.

# THE TRUSTEESHIP COUNCIL

### —A Then But Not Now Thing

The Trusteeship Council was set up to supervise the administration of colonies which had been taken from the losers of World Wars I and II.

Taken from the Ottoman Turks, Palestine and Iraq became British mandates, as did some German territories, like Nauru, Samoa, and Tanganyika. Belgium inherited Rwanda and Burundi; the Japanese, many of the Pacific Islands; and the French, Lebanon, Syria, Cameroon and other African territories. The South Africans got the mandate for what later became Namibia.

Trusteeship developed from the League of Nations Mandate system. Apart from rhetoric, the Mandate system itself was invented to appease the refusal of the United States to allow Britain, Belgium, France, and Japan to take over conquered German and Turkish territories and exclude American interests. So the Mandate system was a sort of compromise colonialism.

Hey, what about the freedom to enslave?!

## Back to the Debating Room

Somehow, many former UN Trusteeship territories and League Mandates kept returning to the UN agenda. Somalia, Iraq, Rwanda, and above all Palestine.

Palestine started as a League of Nations Mandate to the British, who had taken it from the Turks. They were supposed to make it a national home for the Jewish people - without prejudicing the rights of the original Palestinian Arabs.

Needless to say, it didn't work. If they let Jewish refugees in, the Arabs accused them of taking their land by stealth. If they stopped Jews from arriving, they were accused of inhumanity. The Zionists wanted a Jewish State, not a home, and the Arabs wanted their own country.

In 1948, the British told the General Assembly they were giving up, and the UN came up with a plan that was even *more impossible*; they split the country in a way that left huge Arab populations in the Jewish state. The end of the Mandate came in a bitter war during which hundreds of thousands of Palestinians were evicted or fled. Only one state, Israel, was set up.

On 9 December 1949, the General Assembly directed the Trusteeship Council to administer Jerusalem - **but neither side accepted the provision.**

In 1948, the Assembly had passed resolution 194, which set up UNRWA to look after the refugees, and mandated that they should be allowed to return or, if they wanted, to be compensated. As a condition for its membership the following year, Israel accepted this and all other UN resolutions. After half a century Israel **still hasn't implemented them**, and millions of refugees from the UN's first major failure are still scattered about the Middle East (to be continued 1956, 1967, 1973, 2000?).

Even if the reality did not always match the rhetoric, the principle was a breakthrough and the UN Trusteeship Council inherited the old Mandates almost unchanged except the Japanese Mandates were taken off Tokyo and handed over to Washington.

# Who can you trust with a Trusteeship?

The Americans dominated the debate over the new Trusteeship system, just as they had over the Mandates, but from an opposite point of view. Just to add some extra spice, the Soviet Union asked for the Trusteeship of Libya! It didn't get it.

While the State Department was trying to push Trusteeship on all British and French colonies, the US War and Navy Departments wanted to keep the Marianas, Marshalls and Carolines they had conquered from Japan.

These islands had the dubious privilege of the world's "most colonized" status.

Their bewildered inhabitants had moved from Spanish to German to Japanese and now to US control within a half century.

In the end F. D. Roosevelt's last official decision before his death in April 1945 was a compromise suggestion which was adopted. The islands became the Strategic Trust Territory, on which no decisions could be taken except by Security Council - on which, of course, the US had a veto.

Remember, these were not colonies, but territories in which the US was supposed to "promote the political, economic, social, and educational advancement of the inhabitants."

Instead, islands like Bikini and Eniwotek were the site of innumerable American nuclear tests, which devastated the land and caused radiation poisoning in many of the inhabitants.

After the Pentagon had split the atom every which way, the inhabitants split the territory four ways; one became the Commonwealth of the Northern Marianas; the Federated States of Micronesia and the Republic of the Marshall Islands became independent states and joined the United Nations. Palau stayed a trusteeship for many years.

In 1979, the 15,000 Palauans in their 16 federated states voted for a non-nuclear constitutional clause that forbade all nuclear materials from being transported, stored, or used on its territory. Cunningly, the framers of the constitution said that this clause could only be removed by a referendum with a 75% vote in favour.

The US insisted that the Compact of Free Association it had signed with Palau gave the Pentagon responsibility for its defense of the territory, and it claimed it could only do so with nuclear weapons. So there was a fifteen year impasse as referendum after referendum failed to deliver the 75%.

In 1994, a settlement was reached, and Palau was the last trusteeship territory to become independent. Palau became the 185th UN member in December 1994.

That should have meant that the Council could be disbanded, but as suggested by a French delegate, it was kept in in mothballs - to avoid raising the "dangerous" question of charter revision - which may have called into question France and Britain's permanent seats on the Security Council!

# THE WORLD COURT

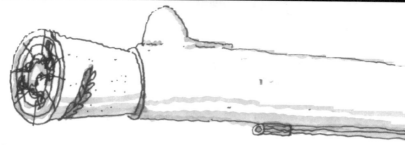

The International Court of Justice (ICJ) was originally set up as part of the League of Nations, and revived as a part of the United Nations. The Assembly and the Security Council vote separately for judges for the 15 strong bench.

The court is fairly small and understaffed, and almost certainly under-used. The idealists set up the court in the hope that its decisions would make war unnecessary, but the countries that refer cases to it tend to be either very highly principled or very, very weak.

The Court is referee in many international treaties, but for disputes between states it needs both sides to accept its jurisdiction.

This is fine - normally. But when the Court found the United States guilty of aggression for mining Nicaraguan harbours, President Ronald Reagan pulled the US out of the Court before damages could be assessed.

This caused some problems when the first Summit of Heads of States of the Security Council took place in early 1992. The first draft called for reference of disputes to the ICJ, but President Bush had been Ronald Reagan's vice president when the US ripped up the ICJ treaty, so the reference was hastily dropped.

So what good is a court without police to enforce its rulings?

Well, it does have moral authority. In contrast to the US's refusal, in 1994 the "outlaw state" Libya withdrew from a strip of territory that it claimed after the Court ruled that it belonged to Chad. On the other hand, the Court also ruled that Western Sahara was an independent territory. The Moroccans didn't agree and have occupied it ever since.

More successfully, the judges delivered the landmark decision establishing that Namibia was still a United Nations responsibility whatever the South Africans said. That led directly - if somewhat slowly - to Namibian independence in 1990.

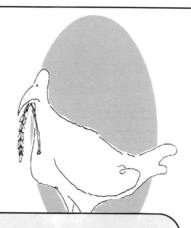

# The Case of the Disappearing Birdlime

When the British acceded to the ICJ treaty, they sneaked in a provision that they wouldn't accept the jurisdiction of the Court for disputes with former colonies and territories that predated 1968. One of those was another tiny Pacific island - **Nauru,** whose phosphate resources had been plundered by a joint trusteeship of Australia, Britain, and New Zealand.

Nauru was a former German colony that became a League of Nations Mandate after World War I. It still upset the Americans, who were not so much concerned about the Nauruans, but the island was in fact mostly bird droppings which made excellent fertilizer.

**To avoid a stink and the claims of the Americans that this was (other people's) colonial exploitation, the three governments formed the British Phosphate Commissioners (BPC) and pretended that it was an independent company.** The BPC dug up a third of the island and sold it to the three governments at way below

world cost. After World War II the island, which had been taken by the Japanese during the war, was retaken and declared a Trusteeship territory.

In the sixties, the islanders petitioned regularly to the Trusteeship Council, and eventually, to everyone's surprise in 1968, became independent as the Republic of Nauru. With a population of some 2,000 it was the smallest state in the world - unless you include the Vatican. The BPC charged the islanders for the facilities it had built on the island, and divided the proceeds among the three colonial governments.

The Nauruans didn't join the United Nations.

Their leaders had seen the Cold War power play at the UN and had decided to stay away. But they did sign on for the ICJ and sued for $300 million damages against Australia, which unlike the British and New Zealanders, hadn't put any small print in its accession to the Court.

The Australians claimed that the court shouldn't have jurisdiction, but after the judges ruled against their technical objections, Canberra rapidly came to an out of court settlement in 1993 totalling some $100 million towards rehabilitation of the land.

## WHERE

### ...Is the United Nations When You Need It?

It's in Geneva, Vienna, Rome, Paris, London, Nairobi and all the other places that have UN Agency headquarters. But these are subsidiaries. The UN headquarters is in New York.

# New York Is for Lovers

Although it hosted the Charter conference, San Francisco wasn't interested in housing the headquarters, so, on St. Valentines Day 1946, the delegates of the first General Assembly met in London and finally agreed to accept the US Congress's offer to move to New York .

Delegates didn't welcome early attempts to site it in suburban New York. You could get suburban life anywhere in the world. So the UN was built on the site of former slaughter houses on land mostly provided by John D. Rockefeller.

In Manhattan, the eighteen acres of the United Nations complex are a sovereign enclave, not subject to US taxation -or for that matter any US constitutional protections.

The famous architect Charles Le Corbusier claimed the design of the UN complex was his - not least the idea of a UN enclave. **"New York is a terrifying city. For us it is menacing. We are not wrong in keeping a distance."**

His claim to be the inspiring genius behind the design is contested by others who give more credit to Brazilian architect Oscar Niemeyer and New York's own William K. Harrison. Perhaps more symbolic than the building was the fact that Niemeyer had difficulty getting into the US because he was suspected of communist affiliations. Corbusier, who'd worked happily with the collaborationist Vichy regime in France suffered no such problems.

His compatriot, Fernand Léger, the designer of the mural in the General Assembly Building, was not allowed in because he was communist, so his designs were executed by an art student.

Of course, it may be totally coincidental that the side walls of the UN building are clad with two thousand tons of marble from Vermont - the state that US Ambassador Warren Austin had represented in the Senate. As an economy measure, the UN's first Secretary General Trygve Lie took six stories off the plans of the building, reducing it to 550 feet.

The General Assembly was originally built for 54 member states. In 1979, it was remodeled for a "maximum of 182 delegations." In 1994, the number grew to 185.

But to compensate, the mini-dome on top of the General Assembly building was reputedly added after Senator Austin told the architects that Congress wouldn't bankroll any public building that wasn't adorned with a capitol-like rotunda.

In keeping with Congressional standards, the ashtrays in the toilet stalls were designed to cope with cigars.

The dome was added and the US made an interest free loan of $65 million, the last installment of which was repaid in 1982, by which time, of course, the great excommunicator Ronald Reagan (at war with the UN) had taken office and reversed the position from the good old days when the Senate had endorsed the UN Charter by 89 to 2.

## Unwelcome Guests

Because it's an international enclave, under the HQ agreement the US has to allow into New York people it wouldn't touch with a bargepole.

So when Palestinian leader Yasser Arafat came to speak at the General Assembly in 1974, Washington was no happier than it'd been when Fidel Castro came (Castro created a stir by staying up in Harlem).

The US was so worried at the consequences of Arafat motoring through the pro-Israeli streets of Manhattan that they asked Secretary General Kurt Waldheim to put him up in the UN itself. The only beds were in the UN

Yassir Arafat and Javier Peres de Cuellar

clinic so he was helicoptered into the UN gardens and put up there.

Kurt Waldheim

*When he was invited back in 1989, the United States broke international law and the HQ agreement by refusing to allow him in. After the US ignored a General Assembly vote of 153 to 2 (guess which two) to rescind the decision, the whole body moved to Geneva to hear him.*

Yasser Arafat and Fidel Castro are far from being the only visitors the UN has. The UN is one of the most popular tourist attractions in New York. It's not the architecture (dull), nor even the exciting people who work there (even duller!). Ordinary people know that the UN stands for something .

49

## The Stamp of Success

In 1947, Argentinean diplomat and General Assembly President Dr. Jose Arce suggested setting up the UN's stamp bureau. The General Assembly finally agreed in 1950, and the UN postal service issued its first stamps in 24 October 1951.

The motivations were prestige, since it made the UN the first intergovernmental agency to issue stamps; propaganda for the UN message - and revenue, since stamp collectors have avidly bought the more than 1,000 stamps issue.

The first commemorative stamps were issued by the tiny landlocked postage stamp republic of San Marino, which had to wait until 1992 to join the United Nations itself.

# HOW?

Collective Action

> "There never was a good war - or a bad peace," said
> Benjamin Franklin in 1783.

But the media know better. Wars make news and hog headlines. Peace treaties, international conventions don't hold a candle to a bloody war for attention. Which is why the UN's many failures hit the screens screaming, while its successes whisper in the small print.

> "There never was a time when, in my opinion, some way could not be found to prevent the drawing of the sword."
>
> -- General Ulysses S. Grant, US President

And the survivors of World War II knew differently as well. They had seen bad peaces turn into worse wars. The appeasement of dictators in Manchuria, Abyssinia, Czechoslovakia, and Spain led to wider and bloodier wars.

### A Fiftieth Anniversary Thought for the UN

> "The world should be made safe for at least fifty years. If it was only for fifteen to twenty years, then we should have betrayed our soldiers."
>
> -- Winston Churchill

So the UN founders were haunted by the idea that strong and early military action would have saved millions of lives by stopping the dictators in their tracks. The UN was not and never has been a pacifist organization.

Its founders wanted it to get its retaliation in first.

And they took many of their lessons from the failure of the UN's predecessor, the League of Nations.

"There is hardly such a thing as a war in which it makes no difference who wins. Nearly always one side stands more or less for progress, the other side more or less for reaction."

--George Orwell, British socialist and author of 1984.

# League of Nations

To see how successful the UN has been, we should look at its predecessor, the League of Nations, which was set up in 1919 to ensure that there'd never be another war after what the survivors optimistically called the "War to End All Wars."

**It failed.**

For a start, although the US President Woodrow Wilson was one of the League's inspirations, Congress didn't share his visions. They blocked US affiliation and thus stymied any sanctions the League may have imposed on aggressors.

In 1931, Japan invaded Manchuria in the north of China in violation of the League Covenant. The League set up a Commission of Inquiry! The invaders continued, and in 1933, the Commission concluded that the invasion was wrong, and the Japanese should get out of Manchuria. Instead Japan got out of the League of Nations and invaded another province of China. Germany, now under Nazi rule, left as well.

In 1935, Italy invaded Ethiopia whose Emperor Haile Selasse appealed in person in Geneva for help, but no one was prepared to back the League Covenant.

One of its main organizational problems was that its decisions needed a consensus of all members, except those directly involved in a dispute. But that was a technicality - the League, just like the UN, could only enforce its decisions if the major military and economic powers were agreed and prepared to act.

On the plus side, the League established the International Labour Organization (ILO) and the forerunner of the World Court, the Permanent International Court of Justice, which both still survive.

With the Mandate system, it established a new principle, that dependent territories were not just to be exploited, but were to be governed in trust for the inhabitants. On the down side - a big one - was World War II.

The League actually snoozed on until 1946, when on 8 April, its remaining members met for the last time to liquidate the organization.

## WHO?

THE MEMBERS *Not an Exclusive Club!*

Groucho Marx once said that he wouldn't want to join any club that would have him as a member. And some of the members of the UN could say the same thing.

Membership is open to all "peace-loving" countries. But that seems to have been flexibly defined to include many countries that would just love a piece of their neighbour.

## Enemy Powers

Germany and Japan had to wait for many years to join, and fifty years later the Charter still called them "former enemy powers."

- Article 107 says that "Nothing in the present Charter shall invalidate or preclude action, in relation to any state which during the Second World War has been an enemy of the any signatory to the present Charter, taken or authorized as a result of that war by the Governments having responsibility for such action."

In other words, Germany and Japan could legally be beaten up on anytime.

In the early days, there was a standoff, with the West freezing out applicants like Albania, Rumania, Hungary, and Bulgaria that it regarded as being total satellites of Moscow. The Soviet Bloc in turn stopped the admission of countries like Spain, which had collaborated with the Nazis and Italy, and also some newly independent countries that it considered imperialist stooges.

MEMBERSHIP TO THE UN....

SORRY FULL!

In 1955, a package deal allowed them all to join, along with Ireland, Austria, Finland, Ceylon, Portugal, and other countries. Japan and Morocco followed the next year. It was not until 1973 that another trade-off admitted both East and West Germany simultaneously. By 1991, even the two Koreas had joined in a similar twinning arrangement. Among major states, that left only Switzerland, whose people keep voting against membership and Taiwan - assiduously blocked by Beijing - outside of the organization.

Swiss membership is raised regularly, and just as regularly defeated by independent-minded Swiss voters, who see no contradiction in raking in the proceeds of the rest of the world's contributions to pay for the second largest concentration of UN offices in Geneva.

# Oddball Members

In 1944 at Dumbarton Oaks conference in Washington, D.C., Stalin's emissaries demanded full membership for all sixteen Soviet Republics, whose independence was, by anyone else's standards, strictly limited. However, he only got membership for two Soviet constituent republics, the Ukraine and Byelorussia.

Stalin was dissuaded from trying to sign up the other 14 by Roosevelt's threat to affiliate for all states in the USA. In the end the West agreed not to oppose membership of the two "republics." Their missions in New York, until the breakdown of the Soviet Union, were their only overseas embassies - and not once did they vote differently from the Soviet Union.

Equally bizarre was China. When the Communists took control in Peking in 1949, the USA insisted that Chiang Kai Shek's government in Taiwan was the legitimate government. So, for over twenty years the rulers of an island in the South Pacific sat on the Security Council, and even used a veto, on behalf of the huge nation which had ejected them. In 1971, the Assembly "restored the lawful rights of the People's Republic of China in the UN."

Although the US went along with this vote, they never forgave the Tanzanian ambassador Abdul Salim Salim for dancing in the aisles in triumph. Twenty years later, it was brought up against him when he was put forward for Secretary General.

Jean Kirkpatrick

Ironically, in the 1970s the Americans insisted that the Communist (but anti-Vietnamese) Khmer Rouges should keep the Kampuchean seat in the General Assembly when they were driven out after some of the worst massacres in modern history.

"A nation is a society united by a delusion about its ancestry and by a common hatred of its neighbours."

-- W.R. Inge, known as the "gloomy Dean" of St. Paul's for his pessimistic view of the world

U Thant said in 1952, "The United States could usually muster a (two-thirds) majority. It was like a one-party system functioning in the Assembly." And so Washington considered the General Assembly a good thing, and it became the major focus of American diplomatic and media attention while the Security Council, where the Soviets had a veto, was relegated to a backwater.

Senator J. William Fulbright, Chairman of the Senate Foreign Relations Com-mittee, was much more forthright.

"Having controlled the United Nations for many years as tightly and easily as a big-city boss controls his party machine, we had got used to the idea that the United Nations was a place where we could work our will."

After 1960, Western control of the Assembly began to slip away. That year, 16 newly independent African states and Cyprus, all joined - bringing UN member-ship up to 100.

By 1976, when the Seychelles, with a pop-ulation of less than 100,000, applied for membership, the US became worried that as many small states became indepen-dent, they would swell the Third World majority in the General Assembly. American delegates began to hint that maybe there should be a minimum size, but that idea came to nothing.

TO BE FILLED

In 1991, the US changed its mind completely - the Soviet threat was gone, and small was beautiful. The US sup-ported the application for membership by Liechtenstein (pop. 30,000), which, of course, had nothing to do with President George Bush's friendship with the Prince.

The smallest state unjoined is the Vatican (800 people on 1/5 of sq mile - very high density but very low birth rate).

# Now you see it; Now you don't - the Vatican

Officially termed the Holy See, the Vatican has it all ways. Its unique governmental form - an absolute monarchy officially elected with the help of the Holy Spirit - is not in itself a bar to membership.

However, some jurists say that a state should have a permanent population, which is difficult for the Vatican to maintain with a state full of continuous but celibate nuns and priests.

That doesn't stop the Vatican from joining in the various World Population conferences as a State, and insisting on consensus, while as a Church it tries to bring pressure on other governments to toe the Pope's unsympathetic line on family planning.

Some small states are resolutely independent. Others' votes are up for sale. Japan's desire to continue whaling has provided an aid bonanza for some small island states, while others have seen successful revenue potential in Taiwan's bid for its own separate UN seat.

It infuriates some bigger members, but since most states subscribe to the doctrines (or fictions) of national sovereignty and equality, they can't do much about it. By 1994, the Alliance of Small Island States could muster over 40 UN members to fight for measures against Global Warming and the sea level rise it entailed.

# The only way you leave this organization is flag first!

In some ways, it's easier to join than to leave. UN lawyers have ruled that states can't be expelled from the organization.

So South Africa and Yugoslavia remained members of the organization even when the General Assembly refused to let their delegates take their seat. (One was under Apartheid rule, and the other was a rump state trying to invade Bosnia and Croatia.) Their flags still flew in front of the UN building. Their diplomats were issued credentials and their embassies released press releases as if there were no difference at all in their status.

61

Only one country ever resigned from the United Nations - Indonesia, which withdrew in January 1965. However, it rejoined the following year in time for the General Assembly, whose President invited it to "resume participation." Others who have left have done so because of unification, like East Germany and South Yemen.

Any state more than two years in arrears on its contributions to the regular budget isn't allowed to vote. Many have got very close to the two-year limit, notoriously the United States, but South Africa was one of the few which went over the limit, after it was barred from voting because of Apartheid. When it was readmitted in 1994, the Assembly decided to forgive its $100 million back dues to help the new majority government.

# What's in a name?

Well, lots. A rose by any other name does not smell as sweet. The strangest example was the admission of "The Former Yugoslav Republic of Macedonia," in 1993.

The Greeks refused to countenance its membership under the name of Macedonia, on which they claimed they'd had a franchise since the days of King Philip and Alexander the Great.

The rest of the world wanted to admit the new country as a hands-off gesture to the Serbs, who had kept the name "Yugoslavia" even though four out of its six constituent republics had defected.

But the Greeks used their blocking influence in the European Union and the US. Hence the oddly named admission of Macedonia as FYROM, whose flag was not hoisted outside the UN while Yugoslavia's was!

## Business as Usual

When the Soviet Union was dissolved, it had been suggested that the loose federation which replaced it, the Commonwealth of Independent States, should take the USSR's seat. But that would establish a precedent for an Italian suggestion for one permanent seat for the European Union, replacing Britain and France.

Andrei Gromyko

Paris and London saw the last vestiges of their post-war great power status disappearing and persuaded their colleagues that there shouldn't be any public debate or discussion. On New Year's Day 1991, the USSR name plate in the Security Council was quietly changed to the Russian Federation - with no official record or announcement.

## Nationalist Fission

By the 1990's, national sovereignty, and even the very idea of the nation state, was looking even more dubious than it had before. Secretary General Boutros Boutros - Ghali lamented that soon the UN would have three or four hundred members. The Soviet Union, Yugoslavia, and Czechoslovakia soon split up, as each minor dialect or religious group demanded its own nation - state. And of course for each state, the definitive test of nationhood was acceptance as a UN member.

"Nationalism is an infantile disease - it is the measles of mankind..."

said Albert Einstein, who lived to see the atom split, but died before Eastern Europe broke out in spots.

# Languages in the Tower of Babel

All official proceedings in the UN are translated into six official languages. Originally these were **English, French, Russian, Chinese (Mandarin)**, the languages of the permanent five and **Spanish**. (Spain was not a member, but all the Latin Americans were.) In the seventies, **Arabic** was added. The oil states promised to pay the cost - and even did for a while. Batteries of interpreters translate conferences simultaneously

between the six languages.

English and French are both official "working languages," but the predominance of English worries the French, who have a regular meeting of Francophone countries in the basement of the UN to attempt to turn the Anglo-Saxon tide. (In many of the countries, like Vietnam, French is spoken by 0.1%, while in others like Bulgaria, their Gallic connection is not only perplexing - it's perplexing in Bulgarian!)

The French supported **both Kurt Waldheim** and **Boutros Boutros-Ghali** as Secretary Generals, because of their fluency in the French language. In fact, as part of the deal for Boutros Ghali's election, for some time after taking office he made half of each speech in French and the other half in English.

The English used at the UN is British English. That's why UN people of *honour* are *recognised* as good *neighbours* whatever *colour* they are and whatever *programme* they are involved in.

The World Bank and IMF people (often alleged to be without *honor* by Third Worlders) are *neighbors* of the Americans in Washington and have Structural Adjustment *Programs* which are *recognized* as devastating developing nations of whatever *color*.

In fact the real language of the UN is UNspeak, a peculiar dialect used nowhere else in the world. Documents and resolutions never use one syllable where six will do. Sometimes it is just bad writing, other times it is a skillful attempt to write around controversial matters without offending 180 plus member states, or to conceal that the organization has failed miserably.

"The inflated style is itself a kind of euphemism. A mass of Latin words falls upon the facts like soft snow, blurring the outlines and covering up all the details. The great enemy of clear language is insincerity."

- George Orwell

It's become a bad habit. Orwell's prophetic book 1984, published just as the UN was starting, described NewSpeak, a form of English in which war was euphemised to peace, and want to plenty. It is widely suspected that this was mistaken for a text book by some UN staff.

# Who Pays?

**You do!** If you pay taxes (and who doesn't?)

## BUDGET UNbalancing the Books

In 1994, the UN system's regular budget was about $6.5 billion a year for over 50,000 staff. With peace keeping, there's another 70,000 troops, and the total budget came to $10.1 billion.

UN officials often claim that the total cost of peacekeeping is less than New York City Police and Fire Departments. And about as effective many people would say. In fact, New York City's total budget in 1994 was $31 billion - three times the UN's. UNESCO once estimated that the world spends more on teaching International Relations than it does on the UN.

Most of the UN's money is raised from member states who pay according to their means. The minimum is 0.01% of the total budget, paid by some 87 countries and equivalent to $102,000 each in 1993.

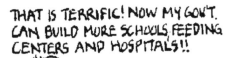

And even that is beyond the reach of some very small states like Niue and Tuvalu.

The maximum, 25%, is paid by the US.

The UN isn't allowed to borrow money. Instead, it juggles money from one account to another, robbing the peacekeeping accounts to pay salaries and so on.

For peacekeeping, the costs of each operation are divided, based on the same percentages. But the Permanent Five pay 22% more for their veto, while the rest pay on a sliding scale down to one-tenth of their assessment for the poorest countries. That means the US pays about one-third of the peacekeeping - or at least it should.

The shortage of money means that it's very difficult to plan ahead, which leads to more inefficiency, which leads to more complaints from the US Congress - although the last thing they'd like to see is an efficient UN!

**In the early years, the US was assessed at 49% of the budget, but as the rest of the world recovered from the war, that was adjusted downwards to 30% in 1957 and in 1974 to its present 25% to the core budget and 31.7% for peacekeeping.**

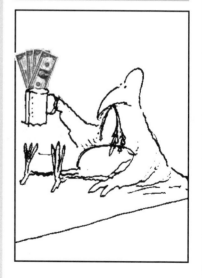

# Zionism Is Racism - or Perhaps Not?

Some of the US opposition to the UN came from legislators who wanted to punish the UN for its Middle East decisions, on which the US was usually outvoted by the rest of the world to two—the US and Israel.

In 1975, at the high tide of Third World power in the UN, the Assembly voted that since Zionism was based upon the exclusive claim of one group of people, it constituted a form of racism, and should be considered such by the UN.

In December 1991, George Bush faced election problems from American Jews over his tough stand against Israeli Prime Minister Shamir. Bush had opposed US aid money being used to build settlements in the occupied territories, so he twisted elbows around the world and had the resolution repealed by 111 to 28.

The Israeli delegation didn't care either way. They stayed away from the Assembly and from Bush's speech, which was, after all, aimed at American political contributors, not them.

True or not, the resolution had given the UN's enemies golden opportunities to attack the organization, but they would anyway, since the UN - often with Washington's support-had often criticized Israeli breaches of international law and UN decisions.

# Is the UN a system?

A Belgian delegate in 1947 described the UN and its agencies as **"a new system of a planetary type: a central organization, the United Nations, around which gravitated independent agencies linked with the former by special agreements."**

Later observers often saw signs of the organization being in orbit.

Dull bureaucrat and first Secretary General Trygve Lie mumbled that the Charter created **"as strong an organization as all of them could agree on and as, in their judgement, could, in practice, be effective at this stage in the history of the world."**

For fifty years the UN agencies and programmes have been growing in a haphazard way, with little coordination and lots of overlap. There are around three dozen separate agencies and programmes - some of which exist just because their staff would hate to be jobless or their host country likes the dollars and prestige of having a UN office. And there are specialized agencies and programmes to suit every alphabet.

1981-1990

# UNalphabetic soup:

IFAD  IMO  FAO  UNIDO  ITU  ICJ
WB  WIPO  WHO  ICAO  IDA  IFC
UNESCO  IMF  UPU  IDA  ILO
GATT/WTO  IAEA  WFP  UNFPA
UNICEF  UNITAR  UNIFEM  ...etc.

All these alphabetical formulae
are supposed to be part of the
UN system.

The heads of the agencies are
separately appointed, are often
in different cities and countries,
and want to do their own thing
anyway, while the Secretary
General has a hard time running
the Secretariat, without trying
to run his far flung empire.

THE LAW
OF THE SEA

"Listen, why don't I have my bureaucrats talk with your bureaucrats?"

As a result, a country that needs UN development aid may find up to 23 agencies, organs and departments each doing their own thing.

Twice a year they meet at the UNspeakable body, the "Administrative Committee on Coordination." It is indeed a committee - but it doesn't administrate, and it doesn't coordinate.

It doesn't have the power to summon agency heads or to enforce its decisions. To disguise this, there is a long - standing tradition that no controversial (read, "important") items should be on the agenda!

All agencies sign "Special Agreements" with the UN. But the World Bank and IMF agreements are very special even by the system's loose standards.

From the beginning, the Bank repudiated any binding coordination with the UN, refused to pledge delivery of information, limited Secretariat attendance at its meetings, and insisted that the UN had no involvement in its budgets. However, that doesn't stop the Bank and the IMF from dictating economic orthodoxy to the rest of the system, as we'll see later.

## Chartered Territory

For all their faults, the UN and its agencies have helped create a genuine world order. For example, **the Universal Postal Union, the International Civil Aviation Organization, the International Telecommunication Union, the World Meteorological Organization, and the Intergovernmental Maritime Consultative Union** are all responsible for allowing global communications on a scale that would be impossible without their coordination. We expect to pick up a telephone and talk to the other side of the world, via satellites in space, or to stick a stamp on an envelope and have it delivered ten thousand miles away.

UN conventions make international law on the use of **space, Antarctica, the sea bed, and latest of all—conservation of "straddling fish stocks."** (Note: Not an ambitious amphibian fish - these are fish which cross international boundaries without a visa.)

UN conventions on Environment, Refugees, Human Rights, on the Rights of Women, of Children, and of Indigenous peoples, like the preamble to the Charter, may often be ignored, but they set standards which governments know they will be judged by.

We can (and we *will*) point to the failures of the UN, in East Timor (200,000 people killed) or Bosnia (ditto), but on the whole it has to be said that **the UN is a good thing. But it could be much better!**

> "This organization is created to prevent you from going to hell. It isn't created to take you to heaven."
>
> -- Henry Cabot Lodge

# THE UN FOR INSIDERS

## Getting Off to a Bad Start - World War Ends, Cold War Begins

About the only thing that united the victors of 1945 was wanting to beat Germany and Japan - and making sure they never posed a threat again. As the last shots ricocheted around the battlefields of World War II, the Cold War began to chill down in a big way and so the new body, instead of being a cozy coterie of veteran allies, split into mutual vetoing.

Within months of the end of the war, in January 1946, Iran asked the Security Council to consider its request for a Soviet withdrawal from the north of Iran, where its troops had been stationed during the war. In return the Soviets promptly asked for the evacuation of British troops in Greece, and Ukraine asked what British troops were doing in Indonesia.

The result was Resolution number 2, which set the pattern for many more decisions which actually decided very little.

> **"The world is divided into two groups of people; the Christian anti-Communists and the others."**
>
> **-- John Foster Dulles**

In the arguments that followed, Soviet Foreign Minister Andrei Gromyko also pioneered what was to become a standard tactic; his delegation walked out of the meeting. (It stopped being standard after the West used a Soviet absence to get the UN involved in the Korean War!)

After the Soviets had withdrawn from Iran in May 1946, the Iranian government asked for its complaint to be dropped. At US insistence the item remained on the Security Council agenda - and stayed there until 1976, thirty years after the Soviets had withdrawn their army and the Iranians had withdrawn their complaint!

It was to be just the first of innumerable items of which the Security Council "remained seized" for decades.

## Making a Korea out of the UN

The first time that the UN took military action was not quite in the way that the founders envisaged - for a start the action was, indirectly, targeted at one of the founders - the USSR.

The Soviets had promised that within a 100 days of the end of the war in Europe, they would attack Japan. They did and in 1945 took Manchuria and Korea in a short campaign. The US and Soviets set the 38th parallel as the division between their occupying forces in Korea.

In 1947, the General Assembly set up a temporary Commission to supervise free elections and oversee the withdrawal of occupy-

ing (Soviet and American) troops from Korea. The Soviets wouldn't allow the commission in - which was not clever, because many of the members were neutral but became prejudiced against the North Koreans because of the refusal. So in 1948, the Commission and the Assembly koshered the South Korean government.

In circumstances that are still the subject of argument, the North and South began fighting in 1950. But no matter who started it, the result was indisputable. The North took most of the South. These weren't great times for Soviet diplomacy. Their delegation was boycotting the Security Council in protest at America's refusal to accept Mao Tse Tung's People's Republic in Beijing as the government of China.

The Soviets were out, from January to August of 1950, and in their absence, on June 25, the Western-dominated Security Council was able to brand the North as an aggressor and order it to withdraw.

They refused to hear the North Korean case, despite an appeal by Yugoslavia, which was then a member of the Council. In fact the absence of the Soviets is convincing evidence either that the North Koreans took action themselves without consulting the Soviets - or that Stalin's foreign service was in total confusion.

The United States moved a resolution calling for all members of the UN to support the government of South Korea, and Britain and France called for the troops to be put under the "Unified Command" of the United States, but authorized the use of the United Nations flag. So the UN flag was used to adorn a campaign over which the UN had absolutely no control. Even now it flies over the Pannumjon border crossing, although the operation has no connection with the UN Secretariat.

The operation also set a precedent for avoidance of the provisions of the Charter about a Military Staff Committee which should have controlled any UN operations. It would have been difficult to have had a Soviet General on the Commission planning operations against its ally!

## Lie and Lie Again

The spirit of the times was represented accurately by the dispiriting career of the first Secretary General of the UN, **Trygve Lie** of Norway, 1946 to 1952, who was described by the British Foreign Office as "a politician, first, last and all the time."

Lie collaborated whole-heartedly with the McCarthyite witchhunt that obsessed the USA in the early days of the Cold War. In 1949, he signed a secret agreement with the State Department and cooperated with Truman's executive order 10422, which violated the UN Charter by requiring a loyalty investigation of all American staff of International organizations.

Any American who was an internationalist, and put his duty to the UN above his duty to American paranoia, was immediately suspect. (To be fair,

there was no chance of a Soviet Bloc citizen join-ing the UN unless the KGB okayed him or her, either). A US Federal Grand Jury found in 1952 that the UN had been infiltrated by "an overwhelmingly large group of disloyal US citizens, many of whom are closely associated with the international communist movement."

American UN staff were denied passports and Lie dismissed forty of them - although eleven of them won compensation, later confirmed by the World Court which defied US pressure.

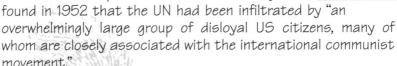

In 1952, the FBI were fingerprinting American staff in the new UN building itself - on international territory, on behalf of the improbably named "International Employees Loyalty Board." Lie promptly dismissed an American staff member who protested at the anomaly.

In June 1953, a plain clothes FBI agent tried to seize a protester from UN guards in the public gallery of the Security Council. Later

that year, J Edgar Hoover told a Senate committee that the extraterritorial status of the UN prevented the FBI from operating on the premises. They *were* operating there, of course, but Dag Hammarskjöld who was by then SG, used the remark as a lever to get them out.

However, the US security checks for staff continued unchallenged until 1983, an American wanting a job with the WHO went to the US courts and got them stopped - because they violated the US constitution! The UN was a passive by-stander in the proceedings. The US government appealed but was unsuccessful, and so the checks finally stopped in 1986 - over forty years after the UN Charter forbade national interference with UN civil servants!

When Lie was first elected, the Soviets supported him - perhaps because as a Norwegian minister he was responsible for chasing Stalin's rival Leon Trotsky out of Norway. By the Korean war, the Soviets were less happy. They boycotted him and addressed all communications to the "Secretariat." In return Lie

*"I'll have a double..."*

ordered his officers not to deal directly with Soviet Bloc countries and to refuse even social invites.

The Soviets then blocked his reappointment, so he was "continued in office" by the General Assembly for three years until he resigned. The revelation of his part in McCarthyite process led to the suicide of the UN's American Legal Counsel Abraham Feller in 1952.

Lie had also allowed the Permanent Five to nominate his deputies, a system that survives to this day, and which allows other countries to use their influence to get jobs for their dead wood, their families or their agents. (This is no disrespect to the bulk of UN staff - who have to carry these parasites.)

"Disloyalty to the Secretary General" became a form of heresy, and as recently as 1993 staff were reminded that rules laid down in the 1950s forbade them speaking to the press. So even the Fourth Estate couldn't bring public attention to what was going on.

# PEACEKEEPING
- UNchartered Courses

By the middle of 1994, the UN was responsible for some 70,000 troops; 2,400 military observers; and over 1,300 police. Peacekeeping costs had almost quadrupled in four years.

For many years - perhaps until the operations in Somalia and Bosnia, the "Blue Helmets," the UN peacekeeping forces, represented all that was best about the organization. They won the Nobel Peace Prize in 1989. When attacked, they usually turned the other cheek. Unarmed or lightly armed, they reminded combatants that the world was watching - and they hoped the world cared.

But there is no provision in the Charter for such forces. A whole ad hoc structure had to be developed to bypass the Military Staff Joint Committee that was supposed to oversee military operations. Instead of the Charter's idea - that the Big Five would stomp on any troublemakers, for many years peacekeepers were not recruited from the Big Five. Neutrals were preferred to wear the distinctive blue helmets and blue berets.

"Peace
is not only better than war, but infinitely more arduous."
--George Bernard Shaw

# The First Blue Helmets

Peacekeeping in the modern sense was invented then, when Britain, France and Israel attacked Egypt in 1956. For once, the USA and USSR agreed with each other. All three aggressors had to get out. It was one of the last times that they agreed and certainly the last time that the US took a strong stand against an Israeli attack.

On 1 November 1956, Canada's Lester Pearson proposed that to enforce the cease-fire there should be...

**"a truly international peace and police force... large enough to keep these borders at peace while a political settlement is being worked out."**

The General Assembly decided to act on his advice. Eisenhower had threatened to cut US financial support from Britain and France, so they reluctantly decided not to object to the UN Emergency Force, as it was called.

(There had been a UN Truce Supervision Force on the frontiers between Israel and the Arabs since 1948 - but they were monitors who checked on events rather than actually stationed on the border.) ·

Brazil, Canada, Ceylon, Columbia, Norway, India, and Yugoslavia provided troops. Since many of the troops wore uniforms similar to the invading British troops, they had to be identified, and so for the first time, the distinctive UN-blue berets and helmets were used. UNEF created another precedent when, despite the objections of many of the contributing countries it was decided that no national flags would be flown, only the UN flag.

Times were different then. The Assembly was dealing with the issue and was considering sanctions on Israel. When Israel refused to withdraw, US President Eisenhower said,

"Should a nation which attacks and occupies foreign territory in the face of United Nations disapproval be allowed to impose conditions on its own withdrawal? If we agree that an armed attack can properly achieve the purposes of the assailant then I fear we will have turned back the clock of international order."

The force was attacked by the American press for not doing things that it hadn't been asked to do and was denounced by the Israelis and the Egyptians in public while privately both accepted it as a good thing. However, the Soviets and French refused to accept its legitimacy and so wouldn't pay for it.

Accepting its pioneering role as expedient scapegoat, UNEF kept the peace for ten years until 1967.

# 1967 War
## *- The Peace That Wasn't Kept*

In 1967, the Israelis attacked Egypt and Syria, while claiming that they had been attacked. Their version predominates. The Soviets, whether out of incompetence or mischief, had told Egyptian leader Gamel Abdul Nasser that there were 12 Israeli Divisions massing on the Syrian border. Nasser asked for UNEF to be redeployed. His Army Commander asked for it to be removed. UN Secretary General U Thant did what he was asked, which provided the excuse that Israeli hawks wanted to get their own back for 1956.

U Thant was widely attacked for agreeing to move out, but legally he had no option. And U Thant did appeal to the Egyptians, but his position was weakened even more when two of the largest contingents, the Indians and Yugoslavs, unequivocally refused to stay if Egypt wanted them to move.

The Israelis couldn't complain because they'd always refused to accept UNEF on their side of the border anyway.

Israel told **U Thant** that it would "not be willing to accept UN discards from Egypt," when it was suggested that UNEF be redeployed to the Israeli side. In the meantime, the Egyptian Army had moved up to the border, which made UNEF's role as a buffer force irrelevant.

The UN's role became the traditional one of scapegoat. The Americans, unable to restrain Israel or reassure Egypt, blamed U Thant. When the Israeli attack started on 5 June, 14 remaining UNEF soldiers were killed. Israel occupied the Golan Heights, the West Bank, the Gaza Strip and the Sinai peninsula right up to the Suez Canal. And this time there was no Eisenhower in the White House prepared to tell them to quit, either directly or through the United Nations.

## The Case of the Missing "THE"

After 1967, long negotiations by the British Ambassador Lord Caradon produced a compromise Security Council resolution, number 242, which ever since has been the contentious basis for a Middle East settlement.

It called for the withdrawal from "territories occupied" in the English text.

It was a deliberate ambiguity since American diplomats envisaged adjustment of the border on the 1948 cease-fire line - not necessarily always to Israel's advantage. The French text referred more specifically to "the" territories, but the English text ruled - or misruled - on this one.

Israel and its supporters have since taken it to mean they only have to give up some of the occupied territories. Thirty years later the issue is still under debate.

# The Congo

The UN was involved in a civil war for the first time in the Congo, now Zaire, in 1960. Left woefully ill-prepared for independence by Belgium, the country began to fall apart almost immediately. There was not one African officer in the armed forces, and there were only sixteen graduates in the country.

The troops saw no reason to continue obeying the Belgians after independence, and mutinies and secessions accompanied a breakdown of the infrastructure. The President and Prime Minister invoked UN aid, and for the first time, **Dag Hammarskjöld** (above) used the Secretary General's powers under article 99 to bring the situation to the attention of the Security Council.

The Council immediately authorized a whole new force -ONUC. The operation began to run into trouble with the Belgian-supported secession of the province of Katanga. The Belgians stalled at leaving. Secessionist leader MoiseTshombe did not want the UN to enter, and the Congolese government both resented ONUC and wanted it to reconquer the country.

The first UN POW's were Canadian troops in Congo/Katanga who were eventually released into Northern Rhodesia (Zambia).

Western incompetence and Soviet expediency made it the Cold War issue, when Krushchev gave a whole new meaning to putting his foot down - he took off his shoe and banged it on the desk during his belligerent speech in the General Assembly. He wanted Hammarskjöld to resign.

In 1963, UN troops, despite the caution imposed by the US and British sympathizers to the secession, finally cleared up Katanga.

# CYPRUS
## -The Island of Aphrodite, Goddess of Love

In 1960, the British granted independence to a unitary Cyprus that was supposed to represent both Greek majority and

Turkish minority on the island. In 1964, the British threw in the towel and referred the situation to the UN as the two communities effectively split the island. **Ralph Bunche** (left) warned the Canadian Ambassador:

> **"If you go in there, you'll never get out."**

**He was right.** From then onwards the UN was the main conduit between the Turkish and Greek - speaking Cypriots.

In 1974, following a military coup by Greek rightists, Turkish troops invaded and eventually seized one - third of the island.

However the UN force (UNICYP) showed a distressing trait of some UN peacekeeping operations. Often, instead of resolving a crisis, they freeze it. Twenty years later the ceasefire line was in exactly the same place.

Every Secretary General since then has tried to mediate between the two communities, but since no one makes the Turkish Cypriots an offer they can't refuse, they sit pretty on twice as much of the island as their population would entitle them to if it were partitioned.

## The UN: The Golden Years?

For most UN veterans, the time that the UN got closest to what it should be was when **Dag Hammärsköld (Sweden, 1953 - 1961)** was Secretary General.

When he was appointed after Lie's shock resignation, he was Director General of the Swedish Foreign Office. Sweden was neutral, which allowed him to avoid a Soviet veto, although the Chinese (Taiwanese) delegate abstained, because Sweden had recognized Beijing.

Lie himself opposed his appointment, saying that he would be "no more than a clerk," and the Council appointed him, thinking that he'd be just another plodding Scandinavian bureaucrat. **He wasn't.**

"It is difficult to see how a leap from today's chaotic and disjointed world to something approaching world federation is to come about... . We must serve our apprenticeship and at every stage try to develop forms of international coexistence as far as is possible at the moment."

-- Dag Hammarskjöld

He set standards for active statesmanship by the Secretary General which have never since been emulated. He was willing to defy the great powers and welcomed what he called **"the final, least tangible, but perhaps most important new factor in diplomacy: mass public opinion as a living force in international affairs."**

He suggested that the job was so demanding that the Charter should specify that its occupant "should have an iron constitution and should not be married." He met those criteria himself - but the response of those he annoyed, like British and French over Suez, was to accuse him of being a homosexual - at a time when this was illegal in many countries.

After the Congo, when Krushchev called for his resignation, Hammarskjöld's reply to the General Assembly brought a standing ovation:

"It is very easy to resign; it is not so easy to stay on. It is very easy to bow to the wish of a big power. It is another matter to resist. As is well known to all Members of this Assembly, I have done so before on many occasions and in many directions. If it is the wish of those nations who see in the Organization their best protection in the present world, I shall now do so again."

**Nikita Khrushchev**

Unfortunately that type of vision leached away. It was shared by U Thant, his successor but perhaps not articulated as loudly. From then on Secretaries General tended to have all the charisma one would expect of a village post office counter clerk.

To Hammarskjöld's credit, he was prepared to get up the nostrils of the White House and the Kremlin. Just before his death, he was disgusted that the US, not for the first or last time, had voted for a resolution then condemned the consequences of what they'd voted for.

Hammarskjöld wrote,

"It is better for the UN to lose the support of the US because it is faithful to law and principles than to survive as an agent whose activities are geared to political purposes never avowed or laid down by the major organs of the UN".

It was a message that later SGs often seemed to forget.
In 1961, the plane Hammarskjöld was flying from the Congo crashed and with it many of the hopes of the UN for a forthright and honest role in world affairs.

# Iran and Iraq War - the First Gulf War

Susan David

In 1980, the forgotten Gulf War began. Iraq's Saddam Hussein took advantage of the confusion caused by the fall of the Shah in Iran to invade and reclaim territories which he had earlier given up. The war lasted almost a decade and killed hundreds of thousands in a war of attrition which recalled the battles of the First World War.

But it was mostly forgotten because the West disliked both parties and wanted to see them weakening each other.

*"Actually, I have no problem beating my swords into ploush shares, so long as I get to keep my AK-47..."*

It also helped that both sides were paying premium prices for the arms produced by all the industrialized powers. Even the Israelis and Americans were selling arms to the Ayatollah, whom they professed as arch enemy.

So what did the Security Council do when faced with absolute proof of Iraqi aggression against Iran? It did nothing. Its resolution did not call for a return to the status quo, since Iran had few friends on the Council at the time.

Brian Urquhart, long-time Under Secretary General, wrote during one fruitless meeting:

> "We are the Awesome Organ,
> A famous sight to see.
> We cannot meet, we cannot vote:
> What bloody use are we?"

Since the war went for the best part of a decade, he was entirely right to ask the question. It's a shame no one's ever got round to answering it.

## U Thant, Burma, 1961-71

The UN hadn't been much more effective during the Vietnam War. But Hammarskjöld's successor U Thant got it in the neck for trying.

## Up in the Stars

U Thant was the permanent representative of Burma to the United Nations - and one of Hammarskjöld's own suggestions as successor. He was the first Third World SG, which helped the Russians agree to him.

UN decision-making processes are often mysterious, but U Thant raised them to new heights of inscrutability, since he also believed in astrology, claiming that he'd foretold the decision of US President Lyndon Baines Johnson to step down in 1968 *because of the movements of Saturn.*

U Thant wrestled bravely but vainly on the Vietnam War, meeting intransigence from Washington which severely strained relations between the UN and the White House -where Mars, the God of War, was definitely in the ascendant.

U Thant was exhausted by the effort of being in middle, but he was extremely accurate in one forecast, when he said,

> **"This widening gap in economic progress between the wealthy and the poor [is] ultimately more explosive than political or ideological differences."**

When he retired, exhausted, he was replaced by **Kurt Waldheim**, perhaps the most ethically challenged SG of all. He'll take some swallowing - so we'll come back to him later.

# THE GULF WAR, 1990-1991

When Iraq invaded Kuwait in 1990, the UN acted promptly to reverse an invasion of a member state. From one point of view this was a text book example of how the UN was supposed to operate. It's just that it didn't usually, so it was like Sherlock Holmes' case of the "Dog That Didn't Bark" - except in this case, the dog did bark, while normally it kept its toothless gums pressed together.

The textbook steps were followed - **diplomatic persuasion followed by the leverage of sanctions, and then, as a last resort, collective military action**. Of course, this time the dog barked for its dinner - a huge bone since Kuwait was floating on a sea of oil and had an ocean of petrodollars sloshing round the Western banking system. Even so, if Iraqi leader Saddam Hussein had had the good sense to hold elections and withdraw, he would have probably had a friendly state on his doorstep.

WHILE DOGGY SLEEPS....

But since he didn't have elections at home, and was not known for tact, he soon dissolved the puppet government he'd set up in Kuwait, and annexed it.

In fact, usually, the UN demands an immediate cease-fire - **which is usually to the advantage of the aggressor, since it leaves him in possession of whatever he has taken.** As a result, the world is littered with uneasy UN-monitored cease-fire lines.

Sheikh Jaber Al-Ahmad Al Jaber Al Sabah, the Emir of Kuwait

But in this case the cease fire line was on the Saudi border, leaving the whole of Kuwait behind it. So the UN immediately imposed sanctions. Saddam Hussein shouted bravado and defiance, while under the table, at the last minute, he put out feelers for negotiations. It was obvious even to the meanest intelligence (everyone except Saddam Hussein) that the White House didn't want negotiations. President Bush wanted a quick and overwhelming military victory.

The Security Council, with its members under heavy pressure from the White House on all fronts, had agreed to contract out the UN operation to United States command, pretty much as had happened in Korea. So it was

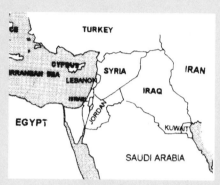

the Pentagon that decided when the war was going to start and finish and how it was to be waged.

Which is why so many people across the world were so disturbed at the intensive bombing of Iraq, especially when some presumed military targets proved to be civilian. Iraqi casualties were huge, while those of the allies were minimal.

Indeed, because the resolutions had no time clause in them, the Iraqis remained under sanctions for years after many Council members would have preferred to see them lifted. The US, UK and France could veto any attempt to lift them.

# NO OIL TO POUR ON TROUBLED WATERS - The UN in the Balkans

Kuwait was weak, defenceless - and oil-rich. Bosnia was weak, defenceless - and oil-less. When the constituent republics of Yugoslavia split apart, they were recognized as independent sovereign states and admitted to UN membership in 1992, which should have guaranteed them all the protection of other member states, like Kuwait.

So when the Serbian-dominated Yugoslav Army attacked, the Security Council decided it was a case of aggression and invoked sanctions against Serbia. But when the Bosnian government asked UN monitors on the frontier with Serbia, they were turned down, because there was no precedent for "preemptive" peacekeeping. Serb military and supplies poured across the border and soon major population centres like Sarajevo were under siege, their civilians shelled and mortared.

It was a clear case for Chapter VII collective action against Serbia, which still kept the name of Yugoslavia. But none of the countries that had rushed to recognize the new Balkan states was eager to provide troops to repel the aggression.

By 1993, the International Court of Justice ruled that genocide was taking place as thousands of Bosnians were killed , raped or deported during what the Serbs called "ethnic cleansing." Under the Genocide Convention that made it a **duty** for signatories to intervene. They didn't.

In the end, governments reluctantly agreed to provide troops for a peacekeeping force whose mandate was originally restricted to safeguarding humanitarian convoys. Eventually, the force had so many mandates that national contingents followed their own agendas. Overall, UNPROFOR, as the force was known, kept people supplied -while the Serbs rained shells on the heads of the people being fed.

ETHNIC CLEANSING! ———

And the forces soon fell into the "peacekeeping mould." They did not distinguish between aggressors and victims or between the legitimately elected government and the would-be usurpers. In fact they treated attempts by the Bosnians to retake "ethnically cleansed" cities as on a par with Serbian attempts to "cleanse" others.

The Security Council was even worse. Before the war it had agreed to a resolution proposed by the Serbs (who represented what was then Yugoslavia) to embargo all arms shipments to the territory. Since the Serbian dominated Yugoslavia had built up huge stockpiles of weaponry, that locked in a big advantage. So the UN embargo was tantamount to tying the victims down, defenceless.

In 1992, 1993, and again in 1994, the General Assembly voted to lift the arms embargo, but the Security Council refused. All the permanent members, except the US, said it would just cause more bloodshed, prolong the suffering etc. After two years of massacres and suffering, they were still saying the same thing!

# On the Horns of a Scapegoat
## Rwanda, Genocide and Inactivity

In May 1994, there were reports of genocide against the Tutsi minority in Rwanda by Hutu majority militia and soldiers. There was already a small UN peace force there, trying to monitor a peace accord between the various factions. It was ill equipped to face such an onslaught and most countries immediately withdrew their contingents.

In New York, the American delegation first supported and then tried to delay a peacekeeping force. The White House was scared that it couldn't get money off Congress, since by then the US was already almost a billion and half dollars in arrears in its UN contributions.

When the Security Council eventually did approve the force, none of the rich countries was prepared to offer troops, and the countries that were had no equipment. The Pentagon charged $12 million to lease some Armoured Personnel Carriers for the Ghanaians, and by the time they arrived the massacres were over. The victim's side was winning the Civil War.

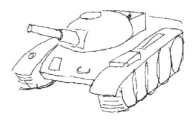

To complicate matters, the French, who'd backed the government doing the murdering, got permission from the Security Council to send their own peacekeeping force. Other members of the Council were profoundly suspicious of the French motives, but the alternative was that they'd have to commit troops, which they weren't prepared to do, and the Americans wanted to avoid a French veto against UN backing for an invasion of Haiti.

The members' suspicions were well founded, the French force ended up defending the fleeing government forces from the rebels, and gave them time to panic the Hutus into fleeing. Millions of refugees poured across the border into neighbouring countries where thousands died of cholera and starvation.

## UNrehabilitated Secretary General

Talk of war crimes, ethics and genocide seems a good cue for **Kurt Waldheim** (Austria, 1972-1981), who was, perhaps, one of the most unlikely candidates for a job associated with Peace and with the defeat of Nazism.

In 1947, the General Assembly had decided that no employee would be recruited who had associations with Nazism and Fascism. The rule disappeared in 1952, and twenty years later,

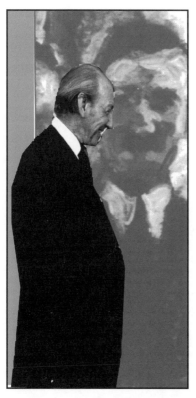

the former Nazi and wanted war criminal became head of an organization which was set up to **defeat the very army in which he served so ignobly.**

His official autobiography lies. It says that after he was wounded in Russia during World War II, he went to study law in Vienna - when in fact he was serving in the Balkans in the Nazi Army, and according to American evidence to the UN's own War Crimes Commission in 1948, he was in the highest category as an "A" suspect for his work there. The army in which he served so prominently did a lot of what became known as "ethnic cleansing" practised later by Serbs.

Somehow, those records sunk from view and the young Waldheim made himself indispensable. Cables from the US embassy in Vienna described him as "cooperative and helpful in promoting US interests."

That may be why, at a time when the FBI was checking the political records of Americans wanting jobs in the UN, the US failed to produce the ample records of Waldheim's war record in its own files. And in 1949, the UN War Crimes Archives, in which he was listed, had been closed to the public.(In fact, not only the great powers found him amenable enough to overlook his war record; the Israelis kept quiet as well.)

He was equally helpful to the Soviets (and others), and in 1971 they sponsored his nomination as Secretary General - with the full support of the powers who had set up the United Nations to defeat the Wermacht.

Brian Urquhart described Waldheim as two different people: one,

"a scheming ambitious, duplicitous egomaniac ready to do anything for advantage or public acclaim;"

and the other, a

"statesmanlike leader who kept his head while all about him were losing theirs."

Waldheim's past made him vulnerable, and his eagerness to please the great powers continued and expanded to include the People's Republic of China when they joined.

However, despite his kowtowing, the Chinese insistence that it was the turn of the Third World deprived him of a third term in office. But, like a stopped clock, he could occasionally be right, like when he said,

"A UN Secretary General has no gunboats at his disposal, only his gifts of reasonable persuasion and skill in negotiation, and the *moral authority of his office* - where it is recognized."

Indeed! The CIA & KGB both presumably knew exactly how much moral authority he had - hence his ineffectiveness!

In 1994, the US made it plain that the former Nazi officer would not be welcome to return to New York to participate in the 50th Anniversary celebrations of the UN the following year. On the other hand, the Pope gave him a papal knighthood.

Although Waldheim did his best to lick clean both his posterity and the posteriors of the great powers, it fell to his "Third World" successor to oversee the end of the Cold War.

# Javier Perez de Cuellar

(Peru, 1982-1991) was the archetypal diplomat. A Peruvian aristocrat, he was an unlikely representative of the Third World, and he was much more at home in Geneva than in Lima. Indeed in his hyperactive retirement, when he was blessed with many directorships, he gained a special residential concession off the Swiss.

When he took office he was self-effacing, almost disappearing into the gray hole on the East River. But he immediately sacked the UN's outspoken human rights director, Theo van Boven, for criticizing some Latin American regimes.

He did indeed work hard to bring an end to the war between Iraq and Iran, without too much help from the great powers, who were happy to see the two Gulf regional superpowers exhausting each other, and his work in El Salvador provided a role model for later democratic peace settlement in Central America.

The end of his term of office was marred by the invasion of Kuwait. During his last year, he was at pains to distance himself - discreetly and diplomatically, of course - from Desert Storm. But, according to the Iraqis, he suppressed their peace overture on the verge of the Gulf War

His report back to the Security Council from the last minute negotiations was cut short - and it was certainly not made public, because even in its

"I'm very sorry, but I'm afraid I really have no idea where you might have lost your sense of moral purpose..."

shortened form it implied an Iraqi offer to negotiate. The White House wanted a quick and successful war - Desert Storm, as the operation was known.

Perez de Cuellar decided not to stand again, pleading his need for retirement. Before he left, his last act was to try to foist on the Security Council a deal over Western Sahara which would have given the King of Morocco almost everything that he would have wanted. Although it was unsuccessful, the Moroccans later offered him a lucrative directorship of a company they owned in France.

COLD WAR ! ——...

In the aftermath of the Cold War, he'd concluded that the world "was clearly witnessing what is probably an irresistible shift in public attitudes toward the belief that the defence of the oppressed in the name of morality should prevail over frontiers and legal documents."

"I have always felt that our primary duty is toward the peoples in whose name the United Nations Charter was written. I have also maintained that whenever necessary we must speak out on matters of principle, regardless of whom we please or displease within or outside the organization."

-- **Theo van Boven**, *Director of Human Rights Commission - who was sacked in 1982 by Perez de Cuellar for speaking out against Latin American governments.*

## "Humanitarian Intervention and National Sovereignty -- A Now and Then Thing

# THE UN FOR OUTSIDERS

## Getting Off to a Bad Start - World War Ends, Cold War Begins

In the old days, the UN intervened in disputes between states. But as some countries collapsed under pressure of civil war, the UN was called in to mediate. The intervention in Somalia represented a major breakthrough for the UN - if not for the Somalis. For the first time the Security Council agreed that the breakdown in a country was sufficient grounds for intervention. Politicians began to talk of "failed states."

The doctrine of humanitarian intervention had been used earlier by the West to justify taking action on behalf of the Kurds in the north of Iraq after the Gulf War. No matter how attractive a concept ethically, it was a very dubious concept in international law. Who decided what was a humanitarian intervention? Could Fidel Castro invade the USA because Americans mistreated black people?

The doctrine wasn't held to be sound at the time and was somewhat undermined when the Germans took over the undubitably Czech areas left the following year.

But in its way, it had a lasting effect on International Law. British Prime Minister Neville Chamberlain's return from capitulation at Munich with his despatch case raised high saying, "I bring peace in our time," went down in history as one of the most fatuous statements in history.

## Genocide

One of the first decisions of the United Nations was to agree a Genocide Convention in 1948, which actually gives a duty on states to intervene to prevent it.

No one ever has.

> **"Thou shalt not kill,**
> **But need'st not strive,**
> **Officiously to keep alive."**
>
> **-- Arthur Hugh Clough, British poet**
> **who exposed Victorian values**

In Rwanda, in Bosnia, in Cambodia, in East Pakistan (Bengal), the great powers stood to one side - or even armed the criminals.

For example, in 1994, US officials were under instructions not to use the word "genocide" about the killing of half of the Tutsis of Rwanda, in case it provoked calls for intervention. They were told to keep quiet about the massacres of Bosnians by Serbs, for the same reasons.

# Khmer, You

## — Cambodia and the UN

During the Vietnam war the United States ignored the United Nations (and the US Congress) and carpet bombed Cambodia on suspicion of harbouring Viet Cong. The CIA helped overthrow the neutralist government of Prince Sihanouk to replace it with a military regime dependent on the US.

That encouraged many Khmers to throw in their lot with the Khmer Rouge (Red Khmers), who took power in 1975. Declaring war on the twentieth century, the Khmers staged killings of class enemies and politically unreliable elements. No one seemed to mind too much - except the victims. But then the Khmers Rouge began to raid Vietnamese border areas.

The Vietnamese swept in and installed a new regime in 1979.

The West, led by the US, and China, insisted for years that the Khmer Rouge were the legitimate government of Cambodia although they controlled only a few redoubts in the jungles on the borders with Thailand.

The US had never forgiven the Vietnamese for winning the war and wanted to bleed them with a guerrilla war on the Eastern flank, while the Chinese had also moved from being wartime allies of Hanoi to peacetime rivals. They wanted to ensure that the Vietnamese didn't have unchallenged power in Indochina.

The Chinese and Americans not only continued to recognize the Khmer Rouge, they armed them for a civil war that lasted a decade, until put on hold, sort of, by the UN peacekeeping operation. With their backing, the genocidal government in exile kept the UN seat until 1990, even though they controlled only a tiny strip of territory on the Thai border.

No one seemed to worry too much about the ordinary Khmers, which was just the attitude that had given the Khmer Rouge their first chance at power.

In 1991, the biggest ever UN operation, UNTAC, almost rebuilt the battered country from scratch, supervising elections for a new coalition government. However, it did not disarm the Khmer Rouge, or force them to allow people in their areas to participate. In 1993, the UN pulled out. The Khmer Rouge didn't.

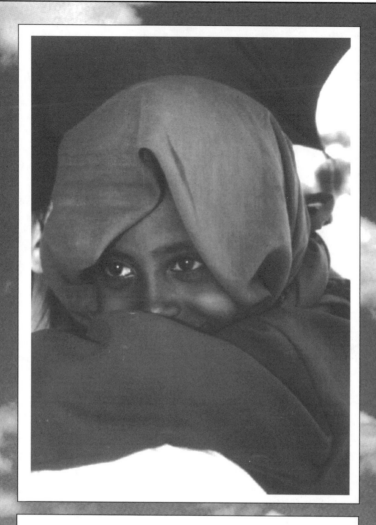

## SOMALIA

Somalia was an extreme case. Of all the nations of Africa, Somalia is the closest to the Western idea of a nation state, since its people all had the same language and religion.

But they were divided into clans and armed to the teeth, since the former government had switched sides several times in the Cold War, and each time their new patrons had shown their appreciation by passing on huge arsenals.

By 1991 the civil war had resulted in the disappearance of the old regime, but left several rival claimants to the new government. Clan militias roamed the cities, sometimes robbing relief convoys while thousands starved.

Boutros Boutros-Ghali, with some justification, accused the West of not caring because it was in Africa and instead devoting their attention to what he called the "rich man's war," Bosnia.

*In fact he took it too far, uttering one of the world's most tactless phrases ever, when he landed in besieged and starving Sarajevo, telling the locals that there were ten places in the world worse off than them.*

The US sent troops into Mogadishu in December 1992. The US marines stormed ashore in full invasion mode. Some of American forces were under UN control , and some were not. Washington refused to do what Boutros-Ghali wanted, which was to disarm the militia, and there were perennial problems deciding who was really in charge.

Scores of peacekeepers were killed and wounded in ambushes and fire fights, for reasons that often seemed mysterious to the victims, although a UN report suggested that some of them resulted from attempts to take on one militia in preference to another.

In 1994, the US pulled out, leaving the militias still better armed than many national armies, and the one war lord whom they made their particular target, free and stronger than ever before. The UN pulled out in 1995, confessing failure.

## Why Doesn't Peacekeeping Work All The Time?

Governments don't always want the UN to succeed when they refer an issue to it. They want to pass the buck, and as Conor Cruise

O'Brien once said, "Failure is really an essential part of the business of the United Nations," adding that members valued "its proven capacity to fail and to be seen to fail."

## Human Rights vs. National Sovereignty- No Contest!

According to the Charter, the UN was to "reaffirm faith in fundamental human rights." Chapter IX calls upon members to cooperate to promote "universal respect for, and observance of, human rights and fundamental freedoms for all without distinction as to race, sex, language, or religion." Somehow the parts of the Charter about national sovereignty are always much more important than human rights when governments get together.

The Commission on Human Rights was appointed by **EcoSoc** (The Economic and Social Committee of the UN) to draw up the **Covenant on Human Rights**. On 10 December, in 1948, the whole General Assembly adopted it without a dissenting vote. Back home governments could dissent all they like, confident that no one would take any action against them.

The 1948 Declaration declares the civil and political rights, the universal right of all persons to life, liberty and security of person, freedom from arbitrary arrest; freedom of movement and residence, of speech, press, assembly and worship. It also invokes the rights of people to economic, cultural and social rights, social security, education, and the right to earn a living.

To celebrate, the USSR started a series of show trials across Eastern Europe, while the US inaugurated the McCarthyite purges during which people were hounded from their jobs and imprisoned for holding insufficiently conservative views.

As we saw, at the UN itself, **Trygve Lie** himself was no slouch in the persecution stakes. Hypocrisy has been a big feature of UN work on Human Rights ever since. In 1968, as Western newspapers carried graphic reports of torture by the Iranian secret police, the Savak, **the Shah** invited U Thant to open an International Conference on Human Rights in Iran's capital, Teheran.

In 1970, the Shah's sister was elected unopposed as Chair of the UN Commission on Human Rights.

Susan David

119

It is no surprise that the Fundamentalists who took the Shah's place are equally concerned about the Human Rights Commission.

**The UN Commission on Human Rights was set up in 1948,** but it wasn't until 1993, at International Conference on Human Rights in Vienna, that the UN appointed a High Commissioner for Human Rights, 40 years after Uruguay first proposed the job in 1951.

He was given some powers of investigation (not too many!). And not nearly as many as he needed, because of the fierce opposition of some member nations.

With his limited resources, he has to implement what's perhaps the UN's greatest achievement, the seventy-plus human rights treaties and covenants now accepted as part of international law.

# 10 December - Human Rights Day
# - A Day in the Life

On 10 December 1993, human rights activists were attacked by the police in Columbo, Sri Lanka, and in Djakarta, Indonesia. The White House issued a declaration to mark the day, while US ships cruising off Haiti picked up and returned refugees who were trying to flee the military regime - which was of course killing anyone who suggested that human rights might be a good thing.

In Bosnia, the Serb Army was shelling Sarajevo, while the Bosnian Croat warlord grandly promised that he would release some of the thousands of Muslims he had interned. Just a normal day for human rights across the world.

The UN operates like the US Congress. When a country moves a resolution in the General Assembly, no one wants to risk losing friends by opposing it, unless there are vital national interests involved - like being leaned on by Washington.

# THE UN FOR WAY OUTSIDERS

### UNFOs - United Nations Flippant Objectives

So in 1979, the Caribbean island state of Grenada moved a resolution setting up a committee to look into UFOs (flying saucers). It passed without vote, because nobody wanted to upset Grenada's old and eccentric prime minister, Sir Eric Gairy, who was an prominent amateur UFOologist. For once the UN Secretariat's failure to act on the resolution led to no angry protests - apart from flying saucer spotters who saw it as part of a conspiracy to hide alien visits from the general public.

*"Go away and come back in 10 years. We haven't set up the committee yet..."*

123

*"Thanks, really, but would it be possible to get an education instead?..."*

More sinisterly, a senior American UN official in 1991 persuaded some Eastern European countries to move a resolution calling on the UN system to support the Institute for East West Dynamics. The organization was backed by the right wing, and virulently anti-UN, Heritage Foundation, whose supporters in Congress and the Administration put heavy pressure on UNDP to make large grant to the organization.

It was of course totally coincidental that the American official involved was about to retire and was to become the paid head of the Institute, whose only address was his own home!

The resolution went through unopposed.

# THE UN CALENDAR - Decadent Decades

*The Nineties!*

People sometimes think that the UN behaves as if it's on a different planet from the rest of us. In fact, it's in a different time warp and has its own calendar.

The 1990's are the **Third Disarmament Decade** and the last week of each October is **Disarmament Week**. It's just that someone forgot to tell the arms producers.

They are also the **Fourth United Nations Development Decade,** which is not be confused with **Transport & Communications Decade for Asia and the Pacific,** which finishes in 1996. Anyone hit by one of the vehicles will surely draw succour from the **Asian and Pacific Decade of Disabled Persons** (1993- 2002).

But it is the **Second Transport and Communications Decade in Africa,** which should not be confused with the **Second Industrial Development Decade for Africa,** which straddles the millennium and doesn't finish until 2002.

In fact it must be party, party all the time in Africa since 1996 was declared the **International Year for the Eradication of Poverty** - and there's a lot of it about in the continent, even with all the Decades!

Stretching out until 2003 is the **Third Decade to Combat Racism and Racial Discrimination,** but capping it the **International Decade of the World's Indigenous People** drags on until 2004 - probably outlasting the people it celebrates.

*"Your card says* 'This year has been declared the UN's year of the indigenous people. Brush off shopworn platitudes, update old sterotypes, and rue, with a heartfelt shake of the head, the genocide upon which our society is based...'."

All across the world, earthquakes and floods are, well, quaking, in the face of the **International Decade for Natural Disaster Reduction,** which was marked in 1994 by the Conference on Disaster Reduction in Tokyo - not long before the earthquake devastated Kobe. 1994 is the **International Year of the Family,** which is followed later in 1999 by the **International Year of the Elderly.**

• **The World Decade for Cultural Development,** which probably saw the final triumph of Hollywood and Disney, draws to a close in 1997.

• The Nineties are also the UN Decades **against Drug Abuse; for the Eradication of Colonialism:** and **for International Law.**

And of course following the **International Year of Sport and the Olympic Ideal** (1994 was marked by shelling of the site of the Winter Olympics in Sarajevo) came the not-to-be-missed **Fiftieth Anniversary of the UN (1995).**

• If this ineffective verbiage gets on your nerves - stop! 1995 is also the **UN Year of Tolerance.**

# OUTSIDERS IN THE UN - SORT OF

*The Misconceived Twins — The World Bank and the IMF*

*"If you go down to Bretton Woods today,*
*You're in for a big surprise - especially if you want help!"*

Article 55 of the UN Charter calls for the promotion of world-wide full employment and the coordination of national full employment

policies. In the eighties the monetarist theories espoused by Margaret Thatcher, Ronald Reagan and the IMF and World Bank made creating unemployment a key to efficiency.

The World Bank, the International Bank for Development, was (mis)conceived, along with the International Monetary Fund at Bretton Woods in New Hampshire in 1944.

The idea was to avoid a repetition of the post First World War economic collapses, which had in part caused World War II. But while at the UN, it's one country one vote, at the Bretton

Woods Institutions it's one dollar one vote. So, as the major shareholder, the US dominates, especially if it was backed by its Western allies.(And it was made plain to them on several occasions that they'd better!)

The two - along with the proposed International Trade Organization, known as the Bretton Woods Institutions, are technically a part of the United Nations system, but the fact that their headquarters are based in Washington is indicative. They use American English and Monetarist economics. And they take little or no notice of what the rest of the UN system, especially the Third World side, has to say.

The IMF was to be a source of temporary funds for nations needing to balance their books. The directors - with the same inbuilt American advantage -- could insist on conditions before allowing aid to be granted. In fact it had invented monetarism even before Milton Friedman.

In the sixties, as a trial run perhaps, it forced the British Labour Government to cut social expenditure as a condition of advancing funds. There was some doubt about whether this was because of concern over what it saw as the Labour Government's socialist policies or retribution for its failure to join the US in fighting in Vietnam - or both.

However, along with the World Bank, the IMF soon pioneered the Structural Adjustment Programs which succeeded in devastating the economies of the Third World.

# LIVING FOSSILS!

Some of the agencies are much older than the UN itself. They represent the history of the modern world.

With improved communications it became important that communications were standardized.

So the **International Telecommunications Union** was founded in 1865 in Paris, as the International Telegraph Union, to coordinate standards and charges for telegraphy. The Morse code was made universal. Soon the organization branched out into telephones and in 1932 took up the allocation of radio bandwidths.

In 1985. this was broken unilaterally by the United States under President Reagan when it set up a TV station beamed at Cuba using wavelengths not allocated to it. Some Americans worried that the Cubans could retaliate and disrupt wavelengths across the Southern USA.

# Knock, Knock! WHO'S Here?

*"Clean water, access to education and health care and a future..."*

There are other famous victories of global action. For example, the WHO has been better at eradicating the scourge of small pox than the UN has been at bottling up the scourge of war. WHO's moment of glory was in 1967 when it set a target of the elimination of smallpox. Ten years later, in 1977 a WHO team moved in on the village of Merca in Somalia and inoculated the inhabitants.

That was the last case of naturally occurring smallpox - unless you count an outbreak in Birmingham in Britain where a laboratory sample escaped in 1978. (The lab-worker who died certainly counted it.)

*"It's positively scandalous, gentlemen! Do you realize that with the $300 million the UN spent on eradicating small pox world wide, we could have bought one nuclear submarine?..."*

The only surviving viruses are in bottles in fridges in Moscow and Atlanta. In 1994, scientists were debating whether it was time for them to go.

In 1994, in Somalia, despite UN peacekeeping and famine relief operations, far more children were dying of war and famine than used to die of small pox.

# The UN and International Law

### Don't fight! Sue!!
### War Crimes - the thousands that got away.

The ICJ only adjudicates on disputes between nations. In 1993, the UN set up a special court to try individuals. The war in the "former Yugoslavia" had seen planned genocide and atrocities that brought back chilling memories of World War II. Across the world, people were concerned that the perpetrators would get away.

Since the West European governments were actually negotiating with some of the criminals - the leaders of the Serbs - this was a well-founded concern. But public pressure forced the governments to do something, even though there were definite signs of footdragging by some of them.

Eventually the International War Crimes Tribunal was established in the Hague, with its own prosecutors and even its own prison cells, leased from the Dutch government.

However, it had to rely on other governments to arrest and deliver the accused. By November 1994, the Tribunal was extraditing **one** Serb suspect from Germany (for 200,000 plus murders!)- but by then, following similar massacres in Rwanda, the Security Council set up a similar Tribunal to try the perpetrators from there. No one was holding their breath. In the meantime, the UN was still negotiating with the war criminals in the Balkans.

But it was a start.

*"Around here, you have to worry about the mosquitos, the waterborne diseases and, of course, the adults..."*

# MAKING WAVES

In the 1940's the UN was granted its own New York Radio Frequency, so it could tell the locals the good news. (The natives were much friendlier in those days!) It lent the frequency to Fordham University.

When it was approached in 1994, the University decided that it didn't want to hand it back. But the UN does make its own radio and TV shows which are distributed free and seen and heard by millions across the world.

*"Evolution"*

# The Big Bang and the Origins of the UN

The First Session of the General Assembly took place a few months after the dropping of Atom bombs on Hiroshima and Nagasaki. The delegates unanimously suggested setting up an Atomic Energy Commission which called for enforcement of controls - without a veto.

The outvoted Soviets saw this as a means of stopping them getting parity with the US. In return for controls Stalin called for outlawing of the bomb. It got nowhere, although almost twenty years later, in 1963 popular uproar at the amount of fallout led to the Test Ban Treaty which stopped surface tests for Britain, the USA, and USSR.

# The International Atomic Energy Agency (IAEA)..

In 1953 US President Eisenhower proposed an Atoms for Peace programme and the following year saw the birth of IAEA, which some saw as a hucksterish attempt to sell nuclear power to the world.

*"That's 'Department of **DEFENSE**'..."*

Later the IAEA regained prominence after the Gulf War when it was charged with monitoring Iraq's attempts to build nuclear weapons in defiance of the 1968 Nuclear Non-proliferation treaty.

The UN-Sponsored Treaty only banned *new* nations acquiring nuclear weapons; the permanent five who already had them were not sanctioned in any way except they promised not to help others go nuclear.

Some nations - like Israel - did not sign and so were not liable for IAEA inspections, which fuelled the attempts to develop an "Islamic bomb," by their rivals. **In 1993, the last White Prime Minister of South Africa, De Klerk admitted that his government had developed nuclear weapons, but had since dismantled them.**

Later in 1994, the IAEA was involved when it became evident that the North Koreans, who had also signed the treaty, were developing weapons capability. The North Koreans simply gave notice that they were withdrawing their signatures from the treaty, which they were perfectly entitled to do.

However, unlike Israel, North Korea had few friends left in the world and came to a favourable compromise in which they were given large amounts of aid in return for not going nuclear.

# More bangs per buck

*"Well, I guess this means the soccer game's off..."*

As the UN approached its Fiftieth Anniversary, it was beginning moves against weapons that had killed and maimed more people even than nukes - antipersonnel land mines.

Millions of them were making whole war zones perpetually hazardous. Made of plastic and ceramics instead of metal, they were almost undetectable - until they exploded. In Afghanistan, Vietnam Cambodia, and throughout the battlefields of Africa civilians were killed and injured for years after combat had finished.

In 1992, the UN began publication of an Annual Register of Arms Import and Exports. Unfortunately, governments lie. While hailed as a step forward in Arms Control, the power lies in the Permanent Five of the Security Council - who just happen to be among the main weapons producers and exporters.

# SUCCESSES

We're trying to take a balanced look a the UN - after all it's too big to whitewash. So there are some success stories, in which the UN did what it should and what it could.

South Africa was the scene of some of its biggest successes in reflecting world, not White Washington opinion.

## A Black and White Success Story

UNAPARTHEID

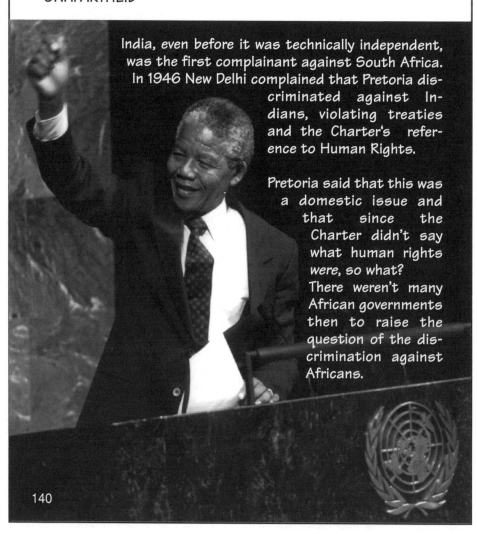

India, even before it was technically independent, was the first complainant against South Africa. In 1946 New Delhi complained that Pretoria discriminated against Indians, violating treaties and the Charter's reference to Human Rights.

Pretoria said that this was a domestic issue and that since the Charter didn't say what human rights were, so what? There weren't many African governments then to raise the question of the discrimination against Africans.

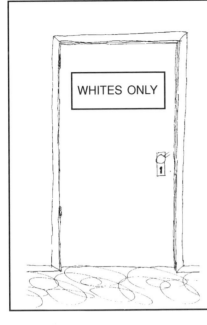

In fact it was raised in 1952 by thirteen Asian states after the South African Nationalist Party introduced official Apartheid in 1949.

Apartheid meant "aparthood" or segregation, but like segregation in the Southern states of the US it was a euphemism for subordination of one race to another.

In 1974, the Third World majority in the General Assembly suspended South African participation in the Assembly. Its flag remained outside the building and its diplomats had full access to facilities. -but they weren't able to vote!

In 1977, the Security Council made an arms embargo against South Africa mandatory. On the one hand, the condemnation of the United Nations helped make South Africa a pariah state - but on the other hand it wasn't until

1994 that Nelson Mandela's accession to the Presidency marked the end of Apartheid and the South African delegation returned to the Assembly. Perhaps against the wishes of some of the permanent members, it was a story in which the UN played an honourable and productive part.

# Namibia

*The one that, almost, got away.*

Most countries accepted that their mandates became UN Trusteeships. However, despite a ruling by the International Court of Justice, South Africa refused to accept any UN role in Namibia, then known as South West Africa.

In 1966, under the influence of the new influx of indpendent African nations, the General Assembly declared the South African occupation illegal and in 1968 renamed the territory Namibia.

It took another twenty years before the White South African government agreed, and even then it was hoping that the UN supervised referendum would go its way. It didn't, returning a majority for the guerrillas, the South West African People's Organization, SWAPO.

In 1990, an independent Namibia entered the United Nations.

Although ultimately successful - it showed one frequent problem with UN operations. Too often, locally based UN officials defer to the strongest party in a contest. And that's not usually the nicest party either.

That was shown brutally when a panicked UN official let one of the South Africa's most brutal commando units out of barracks to massacre hundreds of SWAPO guerrillas returning across the border from Angola.

# Ralph Bunche, 1903-1971: A Good Guy at the UN!

Along with successes, the UN does have its heroes. There are over a thousand staff and peacekeepers who've lost their lives in carrying out UN operations.

But one notable hero role model was Ralph Bunche, the leading Black American intellectual who fought hard against racism at home.

When World War II started, he went into the Office of Strategic Services, OSS, as their main Africa expert, and wrote the training manuals for the American troops going to North Africa. Even so, he was aware of the problems back home and warned about the effect of segregation in the army when troops were sent overseas.

Bunche was on the US team at the London Preparatory Commission for the UN in 1945, with Adlai Stevenson and Stettinius. He was an internationally respected statesman at a time when many of his own people were segregated in schools, stores and even military service. In Washington, he couldn't have ridden at the front of a bus - while in New York he was at the helm of world events.

He once told a State Department colleague:

**"A black man like me, who has a sense of humour, can survive; a black man like Paul Robeson, who doesn't have a sense of humour, takes to wine, women, song, and communism."**

Bunche played a significant part in drafting the Charter itself and mostly drafted the Chapters dealing with colonization and trusteeship - which were its most controversial part.

*"Someday, son, this will all be yours..."*

The first UN personnel forms were copied from American government forms - and included designation for race! Bunche protested and got them changed.

His first assignment was Palestine - as a potential mandate. Bunche drafted both partition plans, and he was made chief assistant to Count Bernadotte, the UN's special representative. When Bernadotte was assassinated by Yitzhak Shamir's party in Palestine, Bunche became mediator and did what everyone thought was impossible - got an armistice agreement signed by all Arab states and Israel.

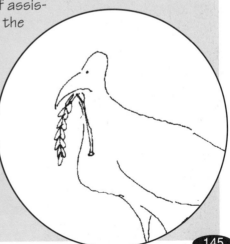

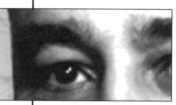

In 1993, two LA street gangs, the Cripps and the Bloods used the armistice Bunche negotiated in Rhodes as the basis for a "treaty" between them.

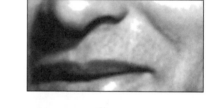

Trygve Lie had to order him to accept the Nobel Peace Prize that he was awarded for his work in the Middle East. In fact, while he deserved it for effort, his modesty was justified.

The Middle East Peace for which he won it was a more elusive prize, still being pursued.

"Take the Peace Prize, dammit..."

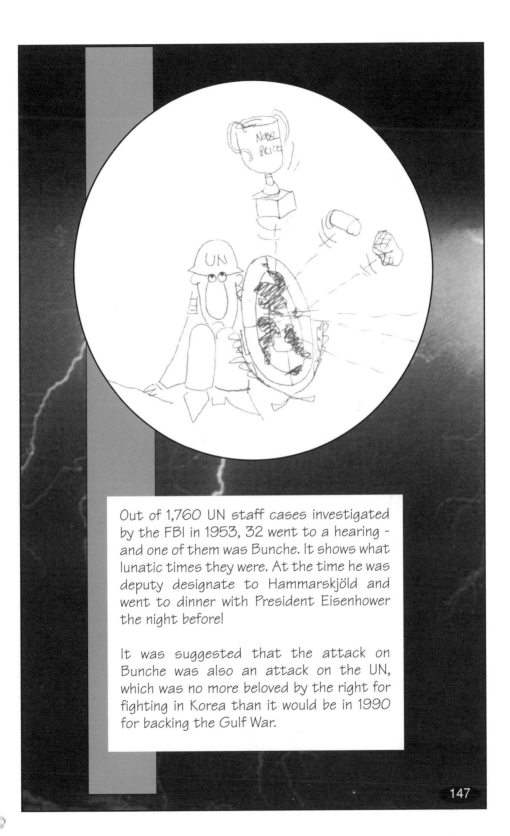

Out of 1,760 UN staff cases investigated by the FBI in 1953, 32 went to a hearing - and one of them was Bunche. It shows what lunatic times they were. At the time he was deputy designate to Hammarskjöld and went to dinner with President Eisenhower the night before!

It was suggested that the attack on Bunche was also an attack on the UN, which was no more beloved by the right for fighting in Korea than it would be in 1990 for backing the Gulf War.

Bunche was a model civil servant. Despite being much respected in Washington, he opposed, sometimes publicly, the American position on Vietnam, Dominican Republic and the seating of Beijing at the UN.

"One does not have to be a pacifist to condemn the napalming and dropping of anti-personnel bombs from 35,000 feet above."

-- R. Bunche

# Who loves ya, baby? The UN's Nobel Prizes

1945: John Boyd Orr
1950: Ralph Bunche for the
         Middle East.
1954 & 1981: UNHCR
1961: Dag Hammarsköld
1965: UNICEF
1969: ILO
1979: Abdus Salam of IAEA
         for physics
1989: UN Peacekeeping forces

## So, is it all worthwhile?

Well, up to a point. The United Nations does represent something that appeals to most people in the world.

It symbolizes the fact that we all live in one world, and that we need to live\ together.

It symbolizes our hope that there are rules and laws that apply to governments.

In an age when someone's car exhaust in Stockholm can contribute to the flooding of an island in the South Pacific;

when a country's economy can be devastated by a few miskeyings on a computer key board;

when a missile can come over any mountain range or ocean;

when droughts, famines and diseases can spread over frontiers as easily as people, fashions and ideas;

then "we the Peoples" hope that the UN can do better in its second half century than it did in its first and give it credit for its achievements -- even if the main one is that there was no World War III -- so far.

"I'd rather regard the UN as a qualified success than an unqualified failure."

-- Brian Urquhart, press conference, 12/7/94

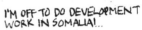

The UN has survived liars and astrologers as Secretaries General. It's taken the rap for the dirty deeds that the Super Powers have wished on it. It's been the scapegoat of nation states great and small.

But if it didn't exist, then we'd have to invent something like it. And if it were reinvented it would probably not look too different from now by the time the governments of the world had their way.

**Eisenhower, UN day, 23 September 1954:**

"With all its defects, with all the failures that we can check up against it, it still represents man's best organized hope to substitute the conference table for the battlefield."

# Can "We the Peoples" do anything to help?

Yes. Take an interest in how your country's delegation votes and behaves at the UN. Don't let them get away with it!

Show that they are being watched. Write and shout. If they make deals in smoke filled rooms, let them know that you'll roast them afterwards.

Complain to your newspapers and TV stations about lack of coverage. If they say the UN is boring, tell them to get better reporters.

It's your United Nations. It says so in the Charter. Rescue it from the gray people in gray suits. Take it back!.

# INDEX

# INDEX